BILL *the* BASTARD

Also by Roland Perry

BILL *the* BASTARD

ROLAND PERRY

ALLEN&UNWIN
SYDNEY·MELBOURNE·AUCKLAND·LONDON

First published in 2012

Copyright © Roland Perry 2012

Allen & Unwin
Sydney, Melbourne, Auckland, London

83 Alexander Street
Crows Nest NSW 2065
Australia
Phone: (61 2) 8425 0100
Email: info@allenandunwin.com
Web: www.allenandunwin.com

Cataloguing-in-Publication details are available
from the National Library of Australia
www.trove.nla.gov.au

ISBN 978 1 76029 009 2

Internal design by Midland Typesetters, Australia
Set in 12/16 pt Adobe Caslon by Midland Typesetters, Australia
Printed and bound in Australia by Griffin Press

10 9 8 7 6 5 4 3 2

To Sheena, who loved her grandfather:
Major Michael Shanahan DSO

With never a sound of trumpet,
With never a flag displayed,
The last of the old campaigners
Lined up for the last parade.

Banjo Paterson, 'The Last Parade'

CONTENTS

1

THE TEST

The recruiting officer at Sydney's Liverpool Army Camp nodded towards the horse corral.

'Break out Bill for Mr Ben Towers,' he said to his assistant.

The merest glance from the assistant back at the officer had the potential new, skinny Light Horseman wondering. He watched as a huge, 730-kilogram chestnut was led into the mounting yard. 'Bill' had a gentle swagger and demeanour yet his size made him imposing. He sauntered behind the assistant. He had a sizeable rump and long back for a Waler, if he was a Waler. His barrel was large, his neck fine and lengthy, and his head was broad. The recruit moved close and reached to stroke his nose.

'Intelligent face,' he mumbled.

The assistant smirked. 'Yeah,' he replied with a chuckle, "intelligent".'

'What's that supposed to mean?'

'Oh, he knows what he's—' the assistant began.

'Saddle him up!' the officer barked, breaking into the conversation.

'Don't need a saddle,' Towers said.

'Okay, Mr Towers,' the officer said, 'mount him.'

Towers did as instructed. He was lithe in his movements. There was grace in his climb, which was more of a slide into position. Towers sat easily, feeling his charge. Bill was still. He seemed disinterested.

'You've come from Cootamundra?' the officer asked.

'Yep,' Towers said.

'Long ride.'

'Yep. Took a few days.'

'There's a recruiting camp down that way. Knock you back?'

Towers' face reddened. 'I . . . no . . . I wanted to see Sydney.'

'First time?'

The recruit nodded.

'Parents know you're here?'

'They died in a fire five years ago.'

The officer scribbled notes. 'Next of kin?'

'Got an uncle, but we hardly speak.'

'His name?'

'Ah . . . Burke. Fred Burke.'

The officer glanced at his clipboard. 'You say you were born in June 1897,' he said, 'which makes you seventeen?'

'Yep.'

The officer and the assistant stepped away.

'Take him round the yard,' the officer instructed.

Towers dug his heels in. Bill remained motionless.

'You asleep, Bill?' Towers said, digging harder.

Bill walked a few paces then bucked hard, his considerable hindquarters pushing high. Towers, surprised, fell forward against Bill's neck, but stayed on. Bill trotted a few paces, then wham! His back arched, his tail flew up high again. Towers fought to stay aboard. Bill trotted on, picking up the pace near the yard's fence. He bucked a third time. Towers, mouthing mumbled expletives, hung on, showing outstanding skill. Bill bucked, kicked and baulked, moving very close to the wooden railing.

'Bastard's trying to . . . throw me over . . . the bloody fence!' Towers yelled.

The officer and his assistant stood well back, observing with amused expressions.

'You got 'im!' the officer called. 'Bloody good. You got 'im!'

Towers fought the reins as Bill continued his furious whirl around the yard a metre from the fence. He bucked every ten paces or so, turning his head towards the fence, making it appear that his intent was indeed to see his rider hurtle into the horse corral.

The officer whispered to the assistant: 'Says he's seventeen.'

'Fifteen tops. I don't reckon he shaves.'

'Nah . . . he's a bloody kid. But he can ride. He sure can ride.' The officer raised his voice. 'Right, Mr Towers, pull him in over here.'

The assistant moved cautiously to Bill's offside to help steady the animal, but Bill was not done yet. He gave one last prodigious leap and kick. Towers was heaved off. He fell hard on his derriere.

'Bastard!' he called at Bill, more in shock than through any hurt, except for his pride. The horse turned his head, looked down at Towers and curled his lip.

'Did you see that?' Towers said. 'He bloody well sneered at me!'

'He's a real sneerer,' the officer commented, 'but he does that to all his victims. His way of saying sorry.'

The assistant led Bill away, his docility returning as fast as it had earlier disappeared.

'You can ride, Mr Towers,' the officer said, scribbling notes on his clipboard. 'How badly do you want to join the Light Horse?'

'It's been my dream ever since I could read,' he said, dusting himself off and wincing as he arched his back. 'Those books on Gordon of Khartoum, the Indian Mutiny of 1857 . . . you know, those yarns about cavalry charges. That did it for me.'

The officer looked up and held his gaze. 'War's not romance, Mr Towers,' he said. 'I was in South Africa.'

'I read about the Boer War . . .' Towers said, still catching his breath.

'Yeah, well, this is going to be a big one, much bigger than that.'

'How do you know? The papers say it could be over by Christmas.'

The officer motioned to the corral. 'We hear,' he said, 'that more than ten times the number of nags will be needed than for South Africa. That means a lot of fighting, a lot of casualties, a lot of dead soldiers . . .' He paused. '. . . and Light Horsemen.'

'Yeah,' Towers said, 'but I'll see the world . . . Paris . . . London . . .'

'Cairo,' the officer murmured, 'Egypt—we hear that's a possibility too.'

'I don't care. I'd see the pyramids. I want to get away from the bush. I'm bored. How else could someone like me get to travel so far?'

'Can you shoot, son?'

'I'm a fair shot,' Towers replied.

The officer looked down at his notes. 'Says here you got second highest score in the rifle test?'

'Yeah, but it was close, one bloke—'

'Hmm,' the officer interrupted, 'how old are you again?'

'You asked me before.'

'But you're older now than when you first told me,' the officer said, holding the recruit's gaze for several seconds before adding, 'why don't you go for a walk around the block and come back a year older?'

Young Towers at first looked confused, but soon understood the instruction. He hobbled off, rubbing his behind ruefully.

'You gunna sign him up?' the assistant asked when Towers was out of earshot.

The officer nodded. 'No one has stayed that long on Bill,' he mused. 'He was up there more than two minutes. And he's a crack shot.' The officer's lean and lined face creased into a grin. 'Must mean he is eighteen.'

The assistant smiled. 'I'd sign him up even if he couldn't hit a barn door at ten paces. Anyone who can handle Bill like that deserves a chance.'

'Bill the Bastard,' the officer corrected with a shake of his head. 'Ah yeah, he lives up to his name every time.'

The recruiting officers only broke out Bill and others like him if they believed the potential recruit was under eighteen, or a pretender from the city who had hardly ridden before. If he was big for his age and his voice had broken, then the officers would test his riding and shooting skills. If he was a crack shot and could stay on Bill or a couple of the other more temperamental horses, the officers would try to assess the recruit's character and then, if satisfied, would let him lie about his age. The youngest 'liar' was thought to be fourteen, even thirteen years old.

If young recruits ticked those five boxes, they were in, at least before they underwent their medical. Males had to be at least 167 centimetres tall with a chest measurement of 86 centimetres. Again, those who proved strong despite not measuring up were accepted, but a recruit had to have good feet. No point in having trouble marching, even in the Light Horse. Mostly, a Light Horseman would dismount and go on foot to a battle. The Light Horsemen were not cavalry. They might ride hard to a battle, then get off and leave their horses with one designated rider. Teeth, too, had to be in fair condition. Dentists would be in short supply, especially in remote battle areas. Colour-blindness was tested but recruits could cheat by memorising charts.

The colour of a recruit's skin was another issue. Since Federation the government had had a 'White Australia Policy', which reached absurd technical depths in army recruiting. Aborigines were not allowed into the forces (at least until later when there was a manpower shortage and many criteria were relaxed), yet those who claimed 'British' family somewhere among their antecedents— even Indians—were taken in.

The acquisition of horses for the two main theatres of war—the Western Front in Europe, and the Eastern Front in the Middle East—was easier. It didn't matter about their background or breeding. They had to be disease-free and strong, which when translated into desert work and battles meant they had to be hardy and durable. The Waler—the peculiarly local horse named for its state of origin (New South Wales)—was the main equine export and featured in the Boer War at the turn of the nineteenth century, when four Australian colonies provided mounted regiments for the first time in a major conflict. World War I, which began in 1914, would be dominated by Walers in the Australian Light Horse force. They usually stood between fourteen and sixteen hands, weighed half a tonne (500 kilograms) on average and were sired by English thoroughbreds from breeding mares that were often part draughthorse. But after many generations the Walers had the benefit of genetic input from the Welsh pony, Timor pony and brumby. This cross-fertilisation had proved useful on the veldt in South Africa, yet no one was sure how Walers would fare in the brutal and hot deserts of the Middle East, if they ended up there. The only indicator was that they often had experience of running wild in Australia's vast semi-arid regions. That had to be a helpful background in coping with a harsh climate.

Bill the Bastard looked as if he had just about every possible gene in his make-up. He was much bigger than the average Waler at more than seventeen hands, which suggested an Arab stallion in the background. There was something of the shanks of a draughthorse, and his legs were long and strong. His sleek neck also bespoke a thoroughbred's genetic input. His eyes were cool yet at the same time alert. Nothing seemed to ruffle him. Instead he ruffled others, especially riders, if he chose. And he always did. There was something in his independent nature that would not allow him to be dominated. His existence was on human terms when it came to his capture and work, but when it came to the rider and mount interplay, he wanted figuratively to be on top, not the man in the saddle. Bill the Bastard had never been fully broken in. In this he wasn't alone in the round-up of horses about to be shipped to

Europe and the Middle East. The army would be relying on hundreds of Australian trainers who would be transported to its remount depots. Their job would be to attend to partly broken-in horses that would have to be worked up to battle readiness.

The recruiting officer commissioned to organise the shipping from Liverpool wanted to hold Bill back. 'No one will be able to ride him,' the officer told his assistant. 'What would be the point in shipping him? Couldn't use him in a charge or any stunt, for that matter.'

'He'd make a terrific packhorse.'

'If they could get anything on him,' the officer said, rolling a cigarette.

'He really only hates riders. I've used him a few times to carry a big load.'

'Hmm,' the officer murmured, lighting the cigarette. 'He is the biggest and strongest bugger I've seen in forty years.'

'I'd send him,' the assistant urged. 'At least he'd give the blokes in the remount section a bit of fun.'

The officer chortled. He liked that thought.

2

THE RESTLESS
TRAVELLER

Bill the Bastard's minder on the 15,000 tonne leviathan
in the Australian flotilla was writer, poet and journalist
A B 'Banjo' Paterson. He had become the disgruntled
figure of his own ballad, 'Clancy of the Overflow'.

I am sitting in my dingy little office, where a stingy
Ray of sunlight struggles feebly down between the houses tall,
And the foetid air and gritty of the dusty, dirty city
Through the open window floating, spreads its foulness
    over all.

And the hurrying people daunt me, and their pallid faces
    haunt me
As they shoulder one another in their rush and nervous haste,

With their eager eyes and greedy, and their stunted forms
  and weedy,
For townsfolk have no time to grow, they have no time
  to waste.

Paterson's narrator dreamt of 'going bush' and living under the stars like his old mate Clancy. But the poet himself was fifty years of age and bored with what he considered to be a struggling humdrum existence. His ballads had brought him fame, and it extended to the UK, where his works conjured outback imagery for the British who had hitherto considered Australia as just a former prison colony. The intensely urbane and intelligent Paterson, with his penchant for bow-ties and bon mots, had created a romantic dimension to life in the Antipodes. He had made his name as a war correspondent for the *Sydney Morning Herald* during the Boer War and even more so as a writer who captured in words the rhythms of the bush and an era in a nation's moods, culture and environment. This was a rare achievement for an author anywhere, at any time.

He was a lawyer by profession, with a patrician's mien, yet he was a poet with a common touch who could deliver simple, compelling bush and city imagery understood by all who read him. The law bored him as much as accountancy did the clerk of his ballad, who *faced the round eternal of the cash book and the journal*. After his South African experience he gave away his law practice, vowing never to take up a deskbound role again. Instead he toured the country lecturing about the Boer War. This kept Paterson's interest up, yet it petered out by 1903 when he was approaching forty. His good connections from his schooldays at Sydney Grammar helped him gain the editorship of *Sydney Evening News*. Paterson once more had a desk, but there was something altogether more stimulating for him in this job, even if he were unsuited to the pace and demands of daily journalism. It allowed little time for reflection, and by nature Paterson liked to go deeply into his mind's crevasses. He stayed in the job for a time before taking on the editorship of the more leisurely *Town & Country Journal*.

After that, he travelled abroad to Europe. His nostrils filled with the whiff of coming war. But Paterson's health failed and he returned home to take up farming. This generated more time for reflection and avoided the 'Clancy' syndrome of city life, but the poet and adventurer remained restless. He married at forty, and this for a time took his mind off the self-indulgent need for permanent stimulation in his professional life. His choice was the attractive and genteel 25-year-old Alice Walker, but the normal restrictions of marriage did not suit him.

Paterson's main frustration was that his true love—writing poetry—paid too little to provide for himself and a family. He spoke of the battle to 'keep ahead of the bills'. Even his wonderful 'Clancy', 'The Man from Snowy River' and the classic 'Waltzing Matilda' brought him a pittance in royalties. This created a sense of cynicism about being so talented yet going unrewarded for it. Artist Norman

Lindsay, who worked for *The Bulletin* as a cartoonist and illustrator, shared something of the same feelings. He described Paterson as 'sardonic' after his decades in journalism, and because of the poor returns for his genius as an original Australian poet.

When war broke out in Europe in August 1914, Paterson had a sudden vision of escape from his permanent state of ennui. He would become a war correspondent once more. He had done it so well before and, besides, the military was part of his heritage, if not his DNA. His great-grandfather, Major Edward Darvall, served under Wellington, first in India and then defending the English coast from Napoleon's threatened invasion. A great-uncle became a major-general in the British Indian Army. (There was a political heritage too. Another great-uncle became attorney-general of New South Wales and a leader of the Sydney establishment.)

Paterson would again be both revived and excited by battle, travel and competing for a 'scoop'. He anticipated seeing London and Paris a second time. This was what he wanted. The thought thrilled him. He rushed to the *Herald* to make a case for it hiring him as a war correspondent, but he was turned down. The federal government, under subtle instruction from the seat of Empire in London, would pick and choose whom it wanted in its propaganda arm, which is how it saw the press. The *Herald* had already chosen Charles Bean to be its reporter. Bean would also act as the official war historian. So much for independent reporting. He had just pipped Keith Murdoch of the

Melbourne *Herald* for the job. The earnest, pedestrian Bean was a good choice. Murdoch was more interested in power than the tedious recording and collating of every event Australia was to take part in on several war fronts. Murdoch instead became the representative of two successive wartime prime ministers, Andrew Fisher and Billy Hughes, when they were not visiting the UK. In effect, he was Australia's official voice in London's halls of power. These quasi-governmental roles were never right for Paterson and he knew it. He wanted utter freedom of expression or nothing. In the end he was left with the latter.

In desperation he turned to his second true love (wife Alice aside), which was horses. He had been brought up in the bush where these treasured and essential animals were a big part of his early life. Paterson could ride almost as soon as he could walk. He was a fair horseman despite an arm deformity caused by an accident when he was young. Horses would help facilitate his travel to war via the barn door. He secured a tenuous role as an honorary veterinarian on a troop ship carrying horses and soldiers. It was a touch humiliating to go to such lengths to escape his 'conventional' life, but Paterson was good on spin. He would write and despatch from wherever the horses went. He would gain insider knowledge and connections. One was the diminutive, well-bred 49-year-old Harry Chauvel, the lean-as-a-ferret, rigid-backed commander of Australia's first ever Light Horse Brigade, which would form part of the nation's 2nd Division. They were nearly the same age, and their paths had crossed briefly at Sydney Grammar.

Paterson's life was re-energised. He went about his new job with the enthusiasm of a keen first-year cadet journalist, writing his first piece as a freelance for the *Herald* called 'Making an Army'.

3

OFF THE DECK

Before Banjo Paterson could revive his career as a war correspondent he had a duty in his role as a would-be vet on board ship in charge of his own horse and a score of others, including Bill the Bastard. Paterson was travelling with 27 qualified vets in the main medical ship. In all there were more than 8000 horses in the 38 transport ships and their minders were kept busy with inevitable equine sickness. Paterson loved his own mount, a sleek, smaller Waler he called 'Trumper' after the cricketer Victor Trumper. But as they steamed into the Indian Ocean he grew fonder of Bill than of any other animal.

Everyone knew the temperamental Bastard's reputation and Paterson was cautious with him. Yet he found an unusual connection. Paterson reckoned this exceptional animal tackled his world in the same way he did his. Bill bowed to no human or thing. Paterson hated bosses or being told what to do. A mutual respect developed. Paterson found himself talking to Bill with more care than he did with any of the other horses. The Bastard in turn didn't kick, but for a couple of occasions, when he was too near. He didn't try to bite him or nudge him out of the way, which he was wont to do with any other vet who came close. The army vets were wary but Bill didn't need anything from them, apart from food and water. When other horses near him had colic, stress or, in a few cases, pneumonia, he remained well.

Bill had caused trouble even before the convoy sailed. He refused to go down to a stall on the lowest of three decks. He leant back like a mule. Four soldiers could not move him. Three pushed from behind and one pulled the reins. Two more soldiers joined the challenge, but Bill was an immoveable object. Paterson was called to deal with it. He suggested Bill was being himself for a reason: the lowest hold was dark and poorly ventilated.

'He has the lungs and heart of an elephant,' Paterson opined. 'I suggest he goes on the top deck. He'd prefer to be in the open.'

Bill was eased up to the top deck, but like a stubborn runner at Flemington, he could not be coaxed or forced into a stall. The ship's vertically challenged adjutant Fred Phillips, known as 'Tom-thumb', intervened and approached Paterson and the six helpers on the top deck.

'If that stubborn bastard doesn't behave, he doesn't go,' Phillips said, pulling himself up to his full 157 centimetres in front of Paterson. 'That's it. I don't want any trouble-makers on board, quadrupeds or bipeds.'

Paterson reflected for several seconds. Staring straight at Bill, he said softly: 'Alright, gents. He hates the fetid bottom deck. He doesn't like the idea of getting splashed on the top deck. That leaves one option or we leave him behind: the middle deck.'

Bill was led down to the middle deck. It was well lit and nicely ventilated. Paterson motioned for the others to step back, then he led Bill to a stall facing across the ship. He was like a friendly labrador as he entered, giving no trouble at all. When he was in and the door closed, Paterson eased around to face him.

'You're a funny Bastard,' he said with a bemused shake of the head. 'Don't know whether you're—to mix my metaphors—a pig-headed mule, or just extra smart.' Bill stared back impassively. 'Maybe you don't know either. Maybe it's all instinct.'

*

A few weeks into the voyage, five horses died within days of each other on the lowest deck. Each time the boat slowed down and the vets slipped a carcass over the side to a watery grave. Paterson was seconded to do it twice. When the seas became rough in the middle of the Indian Ocean, two stalls on the top deck were smashed and the horses in them were swept overboard. All the animals on the top deck seemed in a perpetual state of agitation with waves often washing over them. Paterson wondered about Bill and his choice of the comfortable second deck.

There were deckhands to clean the stalls and feed the horses with oats, bran and chaff three times a day. Each animal was allotted ten gallons of water a day. Paterson looked after only two horses in these chores, Trumper and Bill. He had to do the latter because no deckhand or vet would go into the narrow stall with him. One foolhardy sailor tried but was kicked hard on the shoulder and had to have minor surgery. Paterson felt like a courtier in a tyrant king's throne-room when he slipped in and out of the stall unscathed. There was a terror in it once or twice when Bill seemed in a mood about something. But once Paterson was over his concern, he noticed that Bill sometimes left half of his daily ten gallons of water. This puzzled Paterson. Why would the biggest, strongest horse of the huge contingent drink less than even his small Trumper? Bill ate well enough, but the water was rarely consumed in total. He caused Paterson to think of the hoary old axiom: *you can lead a horse to water, but you can't make him drink.* There was another dimension to Bill, Paterson noted in his diary of the voyage on 3 November 1914: 'You can't lead Bill the Bastard to anything and you certainly can't make him drink.'

*

Paterson was surprised to see a tall, attractive, young fair-haired woman attending to horses on the middle deck.

'Who's that stunning filly with the emerald eyes and diamond smile?' he asked the ship's senior vet, 45-year-old Dr Ian Parsonson.

'She is one of our two lady vets; Cath Phelan from Brisbane,' he replied with a defensive pull at his handlebar moustache. Seeing Paterson's ogling interest as Phelan bent over to examine a horse's foot, he added: 'You're married, Banjo! And she's half your age, *and* taller than you!'

'Maybe two inches at best! Can you introduce us?'

'Tonight at the captain's table, if you wish. But she is engaged to some diplomat named Bob Kerr.'

Paterson groaned. 'Thought she was too good to be true,' he sighed.

'Kath happens to be an excellent vet,' Dr Parsonson said.

'Oh, I am sure she is good at everything she does!'

Paterson was introduced to Phelan that night but it was clear she was not impressed, even when Dr Parsonson said, 'You know he is the famous balladeer?'

'Really? How is he with the horses?' she asked, and ignored Paterson for the rest of the night, leaving him with just the strong fragrance of her perfume, which he could not place. But it was distinctive and appealing. Phelan clung to her tall, handsome, rather aloof fiancé, who was also not forthcoming with Paterson.

When asked about his work, Kerr replied: 'I'm a diplomat,' a tad pompously, as if such a declaration explained everything.

'Aren't we all?' Paterson said, but when this received a wan smile instead of edification, Paterson turned his attention to other diners. Later the captain explained that Kerr was 'some sort of emissary for the prime minister, like the journalist Keith Murdoch'.

Paterson noticed Kerr looking at himself in every reflective surface, even a silver serving dish on the table. It gave the balladeer a sliver of hope that Phelan might just become unimpressed with such a vain figure, whom Paterson hoped was a complete narcissist. Such men, he found, always allowed someone with the balladeer's flair and character, but lesser looks, a chance to compete. But on this occasion, Paterson was left looking on wistfully at the shapely Phelan, whose big sensual mouth and eyes seemed to become larger and more alluring as dinner wore on. Her long white off-the-shoulder evening dress was gathered by a large black belt which accentuated her narrow waist and hourglass figure.

He observed her consuming copious amounts of champagne and chain-smoking small cigars perched in a gold holder. Paterson objected to women who smoked and drank heavily, but he would forgive this sensual, apparently unattainable coquette anything, even the fact that she flirted with everyone except him when her urbane, utterly self-absorbed fiancé retired to their cabin early. Paterson noticed that she was keen to dance, accepting the offers from the best-looking young officers to join them on the dance floor. Encouraged, he invited her but she ignored his offer, almost looking through him as she did so.

Towards the end of the evening, the much-sought-after Phelan, smiling and holding a champagne glass high, swivelled her way to a corner of the dining area and approached a lean, fit-looking, blue-eyed lieutenant who had been sitting alone through dinner, engrossed in a book while the revelry and dancing whirled on the floor a few metres away.

'May I?' Phelan asked as she pulled out a chair at the man's table. The square-jawed, ruggedly handsome Light Horse officer neither nodded nor shook his head as he stood and somewhat reluctantly drew himself out of the tome that was absorbing him.

'Must be a damned good book!' Phelan observed with a grin of full-on charm, without bothering to look at the cover. He proffered a half-nod, his gaze fixing on her as if he was in two minds about engaging her. Phelan thrust a hand towards him at chest level in a manner suggesting that he should kiss it. Instead he pulled it down with a firm handshake grip.

'I'm Cath Phelan,' she said with a smile.

'Michael Shanahan,' he said as they both sat down.

'I knew it!' she said, pointing at him. 'I've been wondering if it was you all night! You're a builder from Roma.'

'Italy?' he asked innocently.

'No, silly, Queensland.'

A smile, or something like it, swept his granite face.

'You haven't changed an iota since I last saw you, what . . . twenty-two, twenty-three years ago?' she said.

'I'm sorry . . .'

'You don't remember me?' Phelan asked with a mock frown. 'But you're forgiven. I was a skinny little kid of thirteen when I last saw you. You would have been a dozen years older, which makes you forty-four or forty-five now, right?'

Ignoring the question, he replied: 'You *have* changed.'

'Our parents were good friends. My father was the local pharmacist.'

'Lance Phelan? I remember. They used to go to Sunday mass together.'

'Good Catholics.'

'Not that good. Mine, anyway. They missed Sunday service quite often.'

'Too busy making babies? You would have had about ten siblings when we left Roma for Brisbane in ninety-three.'

'They ended up having sixteen kids.'

'My God, your poor mother!'

The band started up for the last bracket of dances. People around them were making for the dance floor.

'You religious?' she asked.

'No. I'm an agnostic. A socialist agnostic.'

'My, my,' she said, her tone tinged with derision, 'not just a heathen non-believer, but one with a radical political bent. How absolutely fascinating! I would never have picked it.'

Shanahan glanced at his book.

'Lieutenant,' she said, getting to her feet, 'you must

24

dance with me.' Phelan reached out a flamboyant paw again.

He hesitated. She lunged across the table and closed his book.

'Now c'mon,' Phelan prompted, 'you simply can't refuse me. I've waited for this for almost a quarter-century! You were the most *beautiful* ballroom dancer I ever saw.' He stood, still in two minds as she added: 'I used to get dragged along with my siblings to the local dance places. I recall watching you in awe and some envy for your partners as you'd glide your way around that old barn at the . . . the . . .'

'MacDonalds.'

'Yes, yes, the MacDonalds. I wished, I *prayed* that you would ask me to dance, but you never did. You didn't know I existed.'

'What a rotter . . .' he mumbled, 'but you know that old Sicilian saying—*beware of answered prayers . . .?*' He took her hand and led her to the floor. They flowed gracefully through several waltzes. Other dancers made room for them.

'You're so brilliant!' she whispered in his ear. She kissed his cheek lightly.

They finished the bracket together. Shanahan accompanied her to her table. Phelan leant close and said quietly: 'I must confess, I had the most terrible, terrible knee-trembling crush on you.' She fixed her gaze on him, waiting for a reaction.

'If only I'd known,' he responded, deadpan.

She stopped short of the table. 'What? Would you have done anything?'

'Perhaps given you a good spanking for being so precocious.'

'I would have enjoyed it—*anything*—from you!'

Phelan let her hand slip from his and he received her most seductive smile of the evening.

The next day, Paterson groomed Bill and Trumper after the midday feed and attended to their feet. In the afternoon, mats were placed on the decks and the horses were walked around for exercise. Bill refused to come out of his stall, and not even Paterson could budge him. 'Wallow in your own bloody excrement then!' Paterson called to him as he left the stall. He jumped clear as Bill kicked back at the door so hard that he split the wood. His minder never abused him again.

On 4 November his diary noted: 'Horses very drowsy. My horse goes to sleep and falls down. I don't realise it until Bill makes such a ruckus two stalls away that I investigate. Was Bill letting me know or just being his bloody-minded self? I don't know. I never know with him.'

5 November: 'Put big horse [Bill] in a sling [hammock]. He went to sleep, lay in the sling and nearly pitched out.'

Paterson became acquainted with a big, muscular American soldier on board who had been in the Philippines War (1899–1902, between the United States and Filipino revolutionaries). They spoke about their respective wars, and their current charges. The American had a trick pony which he was 'hustling' about the stall.

'Look out, man,' Paterson said, 'that horse will kill you!'

'No sir, me and this hoss is very well acquainted,' the American said, using his enormous forearms to push the pony aside. 'But you and that big fella—man, you're brave goin' in there with him!'

'I think I am brave,' Paterson agreed, and they both laughed.

'This hoss, he's kinda predictable, even the way he kicks. But that Bill o' yours, you never know with him.'

4

EGYPT

About halfway through the voyage the convoy was made aware that it was travelling to Egypt, not Europe. Instead of gazing up at the triangular elongation of the Eiffel Tower in the crowded metropolis of Paris, the world's most sophisticated city, the lads would be photographing the squat triangular marvel of the pyramids in an almost empty desert. There were no high-kicking French girls in sight or to gossip about, just dead pharaohs inside the pyramids and out of sight. Most adjusted. Many had joined up just for the travel anyway. They were tourists in an unexpected land displaying boisterous ignorance and interest in everything.

Harry Chauvel, who would command the Light Horse, had been in London. He arrived at Maadi, a European suburb five kilometres from Cairo, to greet them. He was a short, thin Australian aristocrat who rode so well that he always seemed grand in the saddle. He was forty-nine years of age and just 'young' enough for service. Chauvel was originally from Tabulam in New South Wales, but later based at his cattle station over the border in Queensland at Canning Downs South. Despite his upper-class mien, his farm background and natural leadership capacity meant he was really born to rule, or at least command. The chance to exercise this was in the military and with the Light Horse. His Boer War experience fourteen years earlier had toughened him. He was determined to make a mark in war at the next opportunity and it seemed to be coming fast. Chauvel, like Paterson, was on a horse at two years of age, and had been on one every day of his life since. There was no more elegant horseman, and he understood his animals better than most and perhaps even with more sensitivity than he did humans. But he cared for both in war and was the type of commander you wished for if you were on the front line. He was not prone to panic or hasty decision-making. Chauvel was more cautious than cavalier. He had an excellent sense of when to wait, pull back or strike.

His men and horses had been on his mind during his recent trip to England. Chauvel did not like what he saw at the training camp at Salisbury Plain, which he likened to Siberia. He diverted his Light Horse to Cairo, where conditions would be far better for everything from equipping and preparation to just existing. There were problems in gaining fresh water, and the troopers grumbled about that with good reason, but it was a minor complaint compared to what would have confronted them in the freezing English winter of 1914–15.

Chauvel's brigade of 1560 men consisted of three regiments, each of about 520 men. He had trained many of the 75 officers, including his second-in-command, the uncompromising but brilliant Major William Glasgow, forty, who had a fine record in the Boer War. There were also men of outstanding quality who would be in war for the first time, including Michael Shanahan. Chauvel had noticed his skills as a leader and horseman early on and had influenced his rapid promotion on merit. Like John Monash, who commanded the other (soldier) brigade in Australia's 2nd Division, Chauvel believed in promoting natural leaders regardless of background or rank. They were confident that in the heat of battle this would count in a big way at every level

Chauvel appreciated Shanahan for another reason. The lieutenant had an uncanny way with animals: he was a 'horse whisperer', although he never actually *whispered*. He spoke softly, understandingly. There was something in his relaxed, non-predatory manner that caused horses to respond to his 'suggestions'. Shanahan neither bullied nor pleaded. He became any particular horse's new best friend. He carried sugar lumps and sweets all the time, but this did not explain even a fraction of his freakish ability with them. They were simply part of his repertoire of inducements and cajolery with the mounts. Shanahan would sidle up, have a quiet chat, pat them in the places they liked best and slip them an edible 'present' rather than a 'reward'.

When asked about this, he replied with a smile and a scratch of his jaw: 'Well, you wouldn't give rewards to your best girl, would you?'

This homily always brought a raised eyebrow and nod of agreement. Michael Shanahan was a practical soul. He gave orders to his men with a little more vigour than he did to the horses, but again without bullying them. If a Light Horseman needed disciplining, he would take him aside and have a fatherly chat for, like Chauvel, he was a generation older than the average trooper. This approach garnered the respect of each man under him. They would go anywhere with him and carry out any of his wishes. Each trooper knew that Shanahan would never ask his charges—man or horse—to go anywhere he would not go himself. The men wanted to show as much courage as him, and that was all he asked. He didn't want heroics. He did want teamwork and a strong bond among all his troopers. That way he knew they would look out for each other no matter what the threat. They knew too he would look after their interests before his own. This carried up the chain of command to both the 2nd Division's brigade commanders, Chauvel and Monash. It seemed to augur well for whatever lay ahead.

*

There were some 8000 horses left with Chauvel's brigade after 220 of them died on the sea voyage, three times the expected attrition rate. The losses were caused mainly by pneumonia, brought on by the overcrowding and lack of ventilation on the lowest deck, which Bill had so aggressively avoided. Some twenty or so of the total lost were washed overboard from the top deck, which once more vindicated his apparent 'attitude' to the uncovered stalls. About 3000 of the Walers were ridden or marched about two kilometres to the Nile for watering. The remaining 5000, Bill among them, were taken to nearby irrigation canals. The idea was to exercise all the equine contingent up to their readiness for mounted work. Even he was bracketed among those that would be ridden, although all the remount section would soon be aware that 'the Bastard' was still some way from being broken in fully, *if* it were even possible.

A problem arose when the feed prescribed by the Australian vets ran out. The horses had to endure Egyptian barley straw (tibben). Bill refused it at first then became a reluctant eater, letting the vets know of his discontent by shaking the feed bag and kicking at the same time. It was his form of protest until oats, bran and chaff arrived.

*

In February 1915, Harry Chauvel called Banjo Paterson to a meeting about his work in the war. Paterson was already writing and sending despatches back to Sydney but most were not being published. He was not an 'official' correspondent. It irked him. Chauvel sympathised, telling Paterson that this was a different 'encounter' than in the Boer War where they had first become acquainted.

'Then I'd better go to a theatre where I can report,' Paterson said.

'You can always work at the remount division,' he was told.

'You think I want to sit in Egypt minding horses while war rages in Europe and somewhere near here?'

'It is a most worthwhile job.'

'Get someone else. I'm a writer first and a nag minder a long way second!'

After a short silence, Chauvel said: 'Just know, Banjo, that you are always welcome here. If you do change your mind I will have you promoted and you can be involved in controlling the remount show.'

'Thanks but no thanks.'

With that he took a boat to England and managed to gain a job as an ambulance driver on the Western Front. That didn't last long. By late March 1915 he was on his way back to Australia, even more disgruntled than he had been before he enlisted.

5

MISMATCH

Chauvel began mounted training when the horses were fit, and Bill was among the thousands of horses broken out for troopers. One large Victorian trooper from Cudgewa on the Victorian border, Gerry Henderson, demanded to be 'matched' with him. Henderson, a close-eyed amateur boxer with a lantern jaw, weighed in at 120 kilograms. He was out of condition. Henderson was told about Bill's reputation for being a little 'rough'. The big man was not bothered when the lean, 25-year-old Sergeant Aidan Sutherland from Golspie, Scotland pointed him out from a wooden hut office near the entrance to the remount depot.

'I've busted bigger buggers than that bastard,' Henderson boasted with a burst of unintended alliteration. 'Has he been broken in?'

'Not completely,' was the cryptic reply from black-haired, dark-eyed Sutherland, who had an almost permanently whimsical look and unruffled manner.

'Either he has or he hasn't.'

'Bit tricky wi' this one,' the Scot said with a slow grin. 'A few have ridden him, but not for long. He's real temperamental. Wants his own way all the time.'

'Ah, there are plenty like that,' Henderson said. 'He looks okay. I'll take him.'

Sutherland pointed to the requisition register, indicating his signature was required. 'I'd advise you to try him out first, laddie.'

'I'm not anyone's "laddie", alright, mate?'

'And I'm not anyone's "mate",' Sutherland replied pleasantly enough, 'except for my girlfriend, alright?'

'Yeah, right, mate,' Henderson said absent-mindedly as he wandered over to the fence near Bill and examined him.

Sutherland laughed. 'Got a wee verbal tic, have we, everyone is a "mate", even people who are not?'

'Dunno what you're talkin' about. I want this neddie, okay, mate?'

'Sure, but as I said, it would be wise to just run wee Bill around the depot for a wee-while.'

'Haven't got time for any "wee-wees", mate. We have to assemble in the desert in an hour.'

'Okay, then, trooper,' Sutherland said, and added with an intriguing smile, 'don't say I didn't warn you.'

Sutherland entered the corral and took Bill out. The horse seemed unconcerned. Then again, he often did.

Henderson made the usual greeting noises, but gruffly, letting the animal know who was boss. Bill hardly blinked. He only turned his head when Henderson produced a short jockey's whip. He flicked a fly near the horse.

Henderson led Bill to a mounting yard where his gear was stacked. He planned his first route march with a thousand other troopers who were being addressed in the desert by Chauvel that day. The word was that the commander had something to tell them about their immediate mission and destination. Bill was tethered to a fence. He looked on more placidly than ever as his new 'master' loaded up with the trooper's kit: a bandolier (trooper's cartridge belt); belt with four pouches; bayonet; wire cutters; 150 rounds of ammunition; rifle; and a water bottle. The last item was about the most essential accoutrement for the day. It was already 35 degrees Centigrade in the shade, and locals tipped it would climb to more than 45 degrees.

Next, Henderson began to arrange other items on the compliant Bill, who seemed to be asleep. On went the military saddle, followed by a haversack containing one carryall with one piece of soap, one towel and one meal. This was wedged between the saddle and the base of Bill's neck. His eyes were wide open now with his body being invaded and covered. An overcoat, waterproof ground sheet, blanket, horse brush pad, mess tin, and a canvas bucket were piled on. A feedbag was looped over Bill's neck and pulled to the side so that he couldn't get at it. This was followed by a picketing peg, heel rope, linking rope, and a leather horseshoe case with spare shoes and nails. The weight on Bill's body tallied about 80 kilograms. Henderson mounted, making the total haul on the horse some 200 kilograms. Bill remained impassive.

Henderson urged him to move out. 'C'mon, get going!'

Bill just trotted a few paces and stopped.

'What the . . .?!' Henderson dug his stirrups in and whipped Bill across the shoulder. Bill shook his mane, as if he found this action most disagreeable.

'I get it. You're Bill the *slow* Bastard!'

Bill started to trot again. Henderson began to dovetail with a score of other mounted troopers heading east of Cairo to the desert near the Nile. Bill became more animated, wriggling his trunk and jerking his neck.

'That's it. Get used to the bloody load, cobber.'

Bill picked up the pace. Henderson yelled with delight. Bill was soon into a steady gallop. Henderson tried to rein him in but couldn't. Bill's pace picked up some more, almost as if he were not concerned at his rider's valiant attempts to pull him up. The horse seemed to be enjoying himself. The exercise appeared good for him. By this time, Henderson was in front of about a hundred other troopers, who were urging him on. Then Bill slowed like a locomotive coming into a station. Inside half a minute he was stock still. Henderson cursed and dug his heels in again. Bill responded with a guttural sound. He rushed forward like a bull, head down, ears pinned back and tail straight. Then he pulled up and bucked, swinging his barrel body to the right and pivoting.

Henderson was a good horseman. Normally he may have been able to control this movement but the weight of his gear tipped him out of the saddle. He landed with a thump in the sand that was heard by all the other troopers. Bill turned and rushed close, almost as if he was going to trample the big man. Then he dug his hooves into the sand, stopping a metre from the squirming Henderson. Bill backed off and delivered a signature curl of the lip. Henderson struggled to his feet fuming. He had landed on his coccyx and was in pain. Bill trotted ten metres away and stopped with his back to his rider, who endured good-natured jeering from troopers swooping by. Henderson cursed the horse and a few mates who called out comments.

'I'd pick you up, Gerry, but you're too big and fat!' red-headed Bluey Harold yelled.

'Thought you could ride, mate!' skeletally thin 'Swifty' Thoms said with a guffaw.

Henderson hustled towards Bill, trying to regain what little dignity he had left, for there were few things more humiliating than an experienced bushman being dumped so unceremoniously.

'Wait you . . . why I oughta . . .!' Henderson snorted. He staggered up to Bill. Just as he reached for the saddle, Bill bolted another thirty metres away. Henderson was left stumbling and nearly fell again. He cursed so hard that his deep voice went up an octave. Bill waited. He still had his back to his rider. When Henderson was ten metres away, Bill took off again, then stopped once more,

39

now some forty metres away. Henderson was sweating profusely under the weight of his accoutrements. He needed a drink, but the water bottle was on the horse. He wanted his rifle, but that too was wedged close to the saddle. In battle it would be slung over his shoulder.

'I am going to stick you!' he yelled, but his sheathed bayonet was next to the rifle. Any animal would have comprehended that this human's tone was menacing and threatening. Bill trotted the 600 metres back to the remount depot, leaving Henderson to trudge his own way back laden down with his gear. Each step sent a searing pain through him.

Sutherland hustled out of his office to greet Bill. He looked to the horizon and could see the gesticulating figure of Henderson shimmering in the heat on the sand. Twenty minutes later he stumbled into the depot, still cursing. Sutherland stood close to Bill, shocked that Henderson was yelling that he would bayonet the horse.

'No killing of my steeds, trooper,' Sutherland said, standing between Bill and his would-be killer. The Scot was no more than 174 centimetres and, while fit, about 70 kilograms wringing wet, which was not much more than half the size of the angry trooper. Henderson tried to brush past. Sutherland put his fists up. They were about to engage in a bout of fisticuffs when Bill took off again. He stopped near the gate to the horse corral. Sutherland hurried over and opened it for him. Henderson, still weighed down with his gear, was left standing, his fists in the air. He waddled towards the gate yelling that he wanted to ram his bayonet into Bill's heart.

'You won't even catch him to retrieve your wee bayonet wi' that attitude,' Sutherland said defiantly.

'Then I'll get me mate's fucking rifle and shoot the bastard!'

'I wouldn't do that either. The commander loves his horses. You'd be on a wee charge and on the first boat outta here back to Australia.' Sutherland allowed himself a brief chuckle, adding, 'Along with two hundred other diggers being sent home wi' syphilis! You can't go sticking or shooting your animal just because he dumps you on your not-so-wee arse. We wouldn't have a remount horse left if every trooper reacted like that.'

The remark gave Henderson pause. 'You gave me the bloody horse!' he blurted.

'You accepted it. I have your signature. Said you could ride anything.'

Henderson gazed into the corral where Bill was having a drink at a trough. 'What about my bloody gear on 'im?'

'I'll remove it and have it sent to your tent by pack-horse.' Sutherland grinned. 'I'll make sure it isn't Bill.'

Henderson's face flushed again but before he could abuse Sutherland, the sergeant added with a conciliatory grin, 'Get over it and I'll buy you a wee drink tonight . . .'

6

THE HORSELESS
LIGHT HORSE

Chauvel broke the disappointing news to his Light Horse
Brigade. They would not be taking their mounts to the
battle zone. Only a few score of packhorses and mules,
and a handful of speedy steeds, would accompany them,
the latter for passing urgent messages or mail. Bill the
Bastard's bulk, strength and endurance meant he would
be in that small equine allotment, but as a packhorse. The
war theatre would be 'somewhere' in the Aegean, Chauvel
informed his bewildered men. He told them that the
terrain of sharp ridges and thick scrubby ravines would
be unsuitable for Light Horse or cavalry action. The men
would be going to the war zone as back-up infantry.

The troopers were disappointed and confused. They
were horsemen, not trained soldiers. Yes, they were mostly

good shots, on average better than their infantry brethren, but the anticipated close combat trench warfare was not what any of them had envisaged or volunteered for. They had in mind open fields or plains. Troopers dreamt of the charge on horseback that had been romanticised and glorified in a thousand books, magazines and newspaper reports since Napoleon's halcyon days a century earlier.

Before any severe disgruntlement could set in, Chauvel had his brigade and another from New Zealand do competitive manoeuvres in the desert, with their mounts. This was to take the troopers' minds off the frustration, made worse by the added news that the infantry would soon (mid-April 1915) be en route to the battle destination. The troopers would come later, if needed. This was further disillusionment. They had always considered themselves superior to their foot-slogging mates. Now they had been relegated to support for them. This was a humiliation too great for some. Good-natured banter between the two groups turned into the odd booze-fuelled brawl in Cairo's cafes and bars.

The fake stunts in the desert were not enough to satisfy the troopers. At night they filled in time with various activities in the city, much of it with Egyptian prostitutes. But that turned sour. About one in four contracted a venereal disease, some of them so badly that they had to be shipped back to Australia. This plus the frequent theft of watches, wallets and keepsakes while troopers were 'horizontal dancing' (as they termed it) with the locals built further tensions.

This came to a head on Good Friday, 2 April 1915, in the Cairo red-light district of Haret el Wassa when a group of diggers and troopers decided to cause havoc at a multi-storey brothel. The Anzacs grabbed the women and their Greek pimps and dragged, pushed and hurled them into the street. The brothel was ransacked. Pianos, beds and furniture were hauled from all four levels of the brothel. The Anzacs then piled up those items and others from the cafes where the pimps congregated, and set them on fire. The bonfire drew a crowd, including hundreds more Australians and New Zealanders who were in the area and joined in the bedlam.

The fire brigade arrived, but the revellers blocked their attempts to douse the flames. The Anzacs manhandled the Egyptian firemen, pushing and shoving them away from the conflagration. Fire hoses were cut. A full-scale riot developed with Anzacs, pimps and firemen brawling as the fire spread. Some Light Horsemen commandeered the fire engines and began driving them around the streets with alarms blaring. British military police (Provos) arrived on foot. The Anzacs formed a solid phalanx in front of the brothel, which had now caught fire. They also set fire to a tavern frequented by the brothel's pimps. The Anzacs threw bottles and rocks at the police, who were outnumbered.

It was just after 11 pm when Shanahan and two friends and fellow troopers, the rangy 20-year-old Sergeant Henry 'Chook' Mulherin and barrel-chested 30-year-old Sergeant Barry 'Bow' Legg, walked out of a restaurant and saw the fire in the distance. They drove to Wassa and pushed through the crowd of onlookers to see about 500 Anzacs in the thick of the mayhem.

'Jeez! What can we do?' Legg asked.

They followed Shanahan, who shouldered his way to a police captain.

'The only way to stop them is to get the Lancashire Territorials here fast,' Shanahan told him.

'Why them?' the captain asked. 'Your mates are out of control!'

'Our blokes get on really well with them; they call them the "Chooms",' Shanahan said, ducking a bottle. 'They won't fight them.'

The captain hesitated.

'Don't think about it, do it!' Shanahan yelled above the noise. 'Unless you want the whole of Cairo destroyed.'

The police captain sent an SOS to the Territorials.

Shanahan then led the other two into the fray. They began pulling Anzacs out of the fighting, but they couldn't stop the brawl, which was spreading like spot fires.

'They're all shickered!' Mulherin yelled. 'Nothing will stop 'em!'

About 200 Territorials arrived in trucks. Shanahan hurried to its bug-eyed, chinless commander, who was deploying his men. They had no impact on the brawling. Looting in the brothel and nearby houses and cafes intensified.

'Threaten them,' Shanahan said. 'They won't fight you. We'll back you up.'

The commander shook his head. 'That could take it to another level, Lieutenant . . .' he said, hesitating.

'Commander, it is at *another level* already.' Shanahan pointed to streets beyond the brothel where fires were taking hold and shop and house windows were being broken. More people were fighting, some tangling on the ground. 'Look,' he said calmly, 'fire a volley of shots. That will get their attention. Then have your men fix bayonets and line up in front of the brothel. We'll talk to the Australians. Got a loudhailer?'

The commander did as advised. His soldiers fired in unison into the air. Shanahan moved in front of the brothel as the Territorials marched into position. Shanahan used the hailer to call for calm, telling the Anzacs: 'Okay, you blokes, you've had your fun, now quit it and go back to camp.'

There was a momentary lull in the brawling near him. 'The Chooms are here. They have to do their job . . .'

Shanahan paused as the commander yelled, his face red and eyes now out on stalks: 'Men, fix bayonets!'

'C'mon, you blokes, break it up!' Shanahan shouted. 'You don't want to fight the Chooms, do you? They're our cobbers. The very best of the Poms. We want to fight *with* them, not against them!'

Despite the Anzacs' alcoholic haze and adrenalin rush from fighting, taking on good friends under orders to use weapons seemed a folly too far. The fighting stopped in the vicinity of the brothel. Shanahan, Mulherin and Legg moved among the diggers and troopers, urging them firmly to leave the area. Locals who had been battling the Anzacs began to peel off and depart into narrow side streets. The Provos started to assert their authority.

Shanahan took the police captain aside. 'Don't make arrests, chief, unless you really must,' he said. 'Don't push them around. It will only ignite things again. Our blokes have a one-in, all-in philosophy.'

The captain took the less confrontational cue from Shanahan. Only a few arrests were made. Soon the Anzacs were wandering away in all directions.

The war could not come quickly enough for all concerned. Commanders Chauvel and Monash wanted to avoid further disruption in Cairo. They were cognisant that all their men were volunteers, and there was only so much inaction they would take before desertion or even mutiny entered their minds. The men just wanted to get on with the action. The locals were also wishing for their departure, having had enough of their culture being disrupted by brawling foreign occupiers.

7

AT ANZAC COVE

'Gallipoli.'

The troopers had never heard of it. Few could spell it and even fewer could pronounce it. But even before their transport boat approached the thin finger of Turkish land running into the Aegean, it was legend to the Australian and New Zealand brigades that made up the 2nd Division—the first 'Anzacs'. The troopers would be joining them. 'Anzac' already had a mystical, proud ring to it, as did the land they would soon be invading.

By 12 May 1915 Gallipoli was 'sacred' ground after seventeen days of fighting the 40,000 Turks ensconced in the heights above the beach at Anzac Cove. The first landings had been made on 25 April. Since then hundreds of Anzacs had been killed in this the first action. British generals running the campaign had never expected the battle to go on this long, but the campaign—a hare-brained, undermanned, underequipped, poorly planned, poorly financed fiasco—seemed doomed to be an inglorious 'bog'. None of the Allied troops, French and British at the tip of the Gallipoli Peninsula and the Anzacs on its coast, had managed to scale the heights and take the high ground. Far from it. They were bound to the beaches where encampment tents—looking like giant mush-rooms—had sprung up at the water's edge.

The troopers were called 'reinforcements'. In reality they were replacements, such was the attrition rate of Allied forces getting killed, wounded and fatigued in uncomfortable if not alarming numbers. Excitement interlaced with fear enveloped them as their boat steamed closer to the dark blobs of Gallipoli's coast and Anzac Cove. They could hear the boom of the big guns before making out the imposing cliff-faces and hills behind them, hills that became shadows as evening set in. Soon they could be seen only when shells from British artillery hit them like exploding fireworks. The troopers watched, their eyes darting here and there as the shells made their marks in an asymmetrical pattern.

The ships timed their advance so they were under cover of darkness as they anchored off the coast. Artillery gave way to rifle fire drowned sporadically by the harsher, more concentrated spitting of machine-guns. Chauvel ordered his troops to wait until the morning before going ashore. They would be preceded by the small contingent of mules and horses, including Bill. For the moment, even he was going with the mob, the prodding, the instructions and the noise.

At sun-up, a tiny beach could be seen. It was much smaller than Bondi in Sydney, St Kilda in Melbourne or Cottesloe in Perth. This sandy, pebbled strip, already the subject of a thousand amateur poems and a hundred artists' paintings, was unprepossessing and made uninviting by the intermittent clouds of shrapnel hovering over it. Cliffs that seemed to merge with steep peaks and ridges on dark, scrubby hills hung over the beach.

The horses and mules were roped in barges, which wobbled their way to shore. They became the day's first target for Turkish snipers, who had barely had their first nip of black coffee before taking up positions. They had been ordered to fire at the soldiers, not waste their bullets on quadrupeds. But the targets were much bigger and more than tempting. Tucked in crevasses out of sight of their officers, the odd Turk disobeyed instructions and took a pot shot at the animal barges. Bill was the biggest horse on board, but there were two other sizeable pack-horses, who were both shot in the head. They crumpled in the boat, disturbing the others. Turkish officers with binoculars noticed the 'wasted' hits and used megaphones to bark orders to the snipers: *Anyone caught doing that again will be shot.* The threat by officers to waste bullets even more extravagantly on their own snipers caused the hidden hill assassins to wait for the troopers' barges.

51

The troopers, led by Harry Chauvel and including Lieutenant Shanahan, slipped into landing barges. All the men were ordered to keep low. Bullets pinged into the water, some striking the barges as they meandered past massive battleships to the shore. Light showers of shrapnel rained down. The small beach was shelled from the right flank. Rifle fire was coming from everywhere, creating a chaotic atmosphere under the face of the steep cliffs. Tents, stacks of ammunition boxes, stores and equipment of all kinds took up much space, with soldiers and animals accounting for the rest. The gangly, tall and strict British Major-General Godley directed Chauvel and his regiments to take over from Monash and his decimated brigade. It had taken the brunt of the fighting and had held the line since the day after the diggers arrived. Godley told Chauvel he would be in Monash Valley. His troopers would man the trenches in this vital defence post. If it were penetrated by the Turks, they would haemorrhage down to the beach. Left unsaid was the certain massacre of Anzacs that would follow. The Turks were unlikely to bother about taking prisoners from among the invaders of their land.

Chauvel left the beach with an armed guard of troopers, including Shanahan. They were followed up the scrubby valley by a single file of horses and mules packed with regimental gear. Bill was the lead animal. His reputation for remaining steadfast in all circumstances except when attempts were made to ride him, saw him given this dubious honour. Monash's engineers had buttressed the valley track with sandbags two metres thick. They were placed intermittently along the twisting path on the left and also on the right at points exposed to sniper fire. Screens of brushwood to hide approaching Anzacs had been mounted on wires. Evidence of Turkish 'successes'— hits on mules and horses—lay rotting in the spring sun. Some of the animals in the train seemed agitated by the noise of shells exploding overhead or hitting the valley walls, but Bill trudged on, his head unusually low as he hauled his 400-kilogram load up the gradient towards Monash Valley, an 800-metre narrow cleft. Its high walls were baked yellow and free of vegetation. Coming the other way past them was a steady trickle of mules carrying dead and wounded soldiers. The path up curved around hills to the most treacherous part of the valley, which was more vulnerable to snipers than any other point along it. This perpetually dangerous valley would be the troopers' 'home' for now.

Michael Shanahan was one of the officers assigned to command Queensland troopers up to the worst possible post at Monash Valley. It was known as Quinn's, after the major in charge. This was the eastern-most post in the valley and had been held ever since the landing on 25 April. Quinn's lay lower than the ridges on either side of it, which made it suicidal for a trooper to raise his head to the level of the trench's parapets either to fire or observe. Worse still, the Turks above them to the left and right could elevate themselves with far less fear of being hit. This gave the enemy fire superiority. Quinn's also had more enemy bombs hurled at it than any other Anzac position. It became the centre of most of the fighting. Other soldiers looked up at it as they would a haunted house. The Turks knew that if they could take Quinn's, they could crash down the valley to Anzac Cove.

The post's precariousness was driven home to the British generals on the beach at the cove on 14 May when General Birdwood, the chirpy, well-respected British commander of both Australian divisions at Gallipoli, was accompanied by Monash and Chauvel up to Quinn's for the first time to have a look at the Turkish positions. Chauvel introduced the general to Shanahan, who briefed him on what he could or could not do in the trench.

'You will have heard of Major Irvine here seventeen days ago, General?'

'Yes, yes,' Birdwood replied briskly, 'he was arguing with some diggers who told him not to stand. He was hit by a sniper. I won't be doing that, Lieutenant, I assure you.'

Diggers and now troopers had asked for periscopes attached to rifles to avoid the fate of Irvine and others. They could aim and shoot without raising their heads above the parapet.

Shanahan handed Birdwood a periscope and showed him how to use it. 'Still keep your head well down, General,' he warned.

Birdwood was using a periscope when a sniper fired and hit the mirror. A bullet fragment struck the top of his head. Birdwood slumped back, bleeding from the scalp.

He was helped down into the valley and stretchered off, a piece of lead lodged in his head.

The cutting down of the commander of the two divisions at Anzac Cove was the lowest point in the siege up until that time. Much to the relief of the Anzac force, Birdwood was up and about the next day with just a headache. But it had an impact on General Godley, who wanted 'swift revenge' on the nearest Turkish trenches. On Saturday 15 May, he ordered Chauvel to make countermoves, whatever the cost. Just as this overreaction was being conveyed to Shanahan and the others at Quinn's, Major-General William Bridges, the Australian commander of the 1st Division, and two senior staffers (Captain Dick Casey and Colonel Cyril White) were three-quarters of the way up Monash Valley. Bridges wanted to stop and a have a cigarette at the sandbag barrier protecting a dressing station just below Steele's Post on the front line west of Chauvel/ Monash HQ. After the Birdwood incident, Bridges was on his way to see the notorious Quinn's for himself. He lit up and moved from behind a barrier back to the path to smoke. He was a tall man, and therefore an easier target for snipers on Dead Man's Ridge, high above him. He had a reputation for being foolhardy and often unnerved his staff by his reckless behaviour, especially the risks he took moving near the trench posts. He chided White and Casey for their caution. Bridges was warned by them to be careful and advised firmly to come back behind the barrier. He ignored them. Seconds later, a bullet struck him in the thigh, splitting open his femoral artery and vein. He was carried behind the sandbags. Stretcher bearers hurried him down to the beach and he was ferried to a hospital ship in a very bad way.

Bridges died three days later. It was another needless waste of a commander when they were in short supply. His body and his big charger, 'Sandy', were shipped back to Australia for a state funeral. Sandy, saddled and stirrups reversed in honour of a fallen division commander, led a parade down Melbourne's Collins Street. Bridges' high profile as Australia's most senior soldier drew a huge crowd. The solemn and dramatic event with Sandy on show provided a sobering contrast to otherwise sanitised reporting on the Gallipoli conflict.

Following the wounding of General Birdwood, Chauvel had no choice but to carry out Godley's impetuous order to retaliate from Quinn's. The troopers were well aware that the nearest Turkish trenches were doing the most damage by fire and bombs on Quinn's and other posts. The no-man's land between the opposing entrenched forces was no more than twenty metres. Any Anzac counterattack would have to negotiate that hemmed-in stretch. Troopers would risk heavy casualties if detected.

'I think this is a harebrained idea,' Major Quinn told his officers when they met at a hut fifteen metres from rope ladders leading up to the treacherous post, 'but Godley wants it done. He is pushing Chauvel. But we just don't know what awaits us. Godley says there are no machine-guns in the nearest trench, but he lied to Brigadier Monash a few weeks back—he told him the Turks had mostly gone down to help their mates at Cape Helles, but they hadn't. They were above Anzac Cove in big numbers and Monash's men were cut down.' Quinn looked into the faces of all his officers. 'I really don't want to command anyone to attempt to run the gauntlet.'

He looked for input from his commanders.

'Under this circumstance, we should draw straws on who commands and what squadron is to be chosen,' one officer said.

Others commented but came to no more definitive solution. Quinn turned to Shanahan, who had kept his peace. 'What do you recommend, Mike?'

All heads turned to Shanahan. At forty-five years of age he was now one of the eldest of the officers and someone who already had shown strong and protective leadership in dealing with the younger troopers. Many of them were teenagers who were unnerved by the experience of being under fire in such a vulnerable position and with very little hope of even effective defence from the post, let alone retaliation. In the space of forty-eight hours, Shanahan had emerged as the embodiment of the cliché: *you would want to be in the trenches with him*. At Quinn's, where nobody wanted to be, including Shanahan himself, his impact on others was paramount. Some officers and troopers were talkative; others were cheerful and kept up morale with comments and jokes to ease the tension; some showed bravado in standing up at Quinn's, an act that had seen a British officer and two diggers killed. Shanahan was none of these. He was the classic example of 'less is more'.

He already had a reputation for taciturnity. Words from him were at a premium. But when he did speak, everyone listened. He had the rare ability of getting to the heart of a problem, including this one put by the troubled Major Quinn. Shanahan took his time before answering.

'We are all volunteers,' he said quietly. 'This should be a voluntary exercise, at least for officers.' He paused and added, 'I shall lead a squadron. But it has to be done at night, not at dawn.'

A few nights later, at 2 am, Shanahan led a silent assault by sixty troopers over the parapet. The Turks detected movement and sent up flares. Despite Godley's certitude about there being no machine-guns in the closest enemy trench, the Turks had a bank of fifteen lined up looking right down the narrow, short slope into no-man's land and then the post. They opened up and mowed down many in the first wave of thirty. Shanahan managed to crawl on his stomach to a rock for cover. He called for the second wave to stay put but his command was drowned out by more fire. He could hear several wounded troopers calling for help. Shanahan bent down and dived towards one, who had been hit in the arm and shoulder. Bullets spat in his direction and kicked up a spray of dirt and dust. A second flare went up. Shanahan lay still and close to the wounded trooper. When the light died he put his body in front of the injured man and manoeuvred him the five metres to the rock. Shanahan again yelled for the second wave of thirty to stay put but his order was once more drowned out. He heard the troopers scream as they charged. The machine-guns opened up again, this time without the benefit of the flare-light. But the damage was still heavy. After an hour, Shanahan was able to ascertain that he had perhaps just a handful of men who were not either killed or wounded. His squad had been decimated, literally. He ordered the troopers to withdraw.

At dawn, Shanahan did the count at the post. Twenty-five men from his aborted mission were dead; a further twenty-seven were wounded. Just eight had survived unscathed. Of those injured, many had terrible wounds from the intense machine-gun fire which could sever a limb. Some fourteen would not fight again.

Shanahan was devastated at losing so many of his squad. The troopers had now shared the morale-shattering experience endured by Monash and his diggers in the seventeen days before the Light Horse arrived. This had been caused by ill-prepared schemes by British commanders who had no concern for soldiers on the front line. Shanahan kept busy, preoccupying himself with looking after the wounded and not dwelling on the deadly folly he had just been through. He supervised their evacuation by a dozen pack animals from Monash Valley until two hours after dawn.

One horse caught his expert eye. He asked a fresh-faced, pudgy medical orderly about it.

'Aye, that's Bill,' the orderly replied as he and an assistant strapped a stretchered trooper on the back of his mule. 'They call him "Bill the Bastard", because no one can ride him. But we've had no trouble with him. One silly bugger at the cove did try to mount him for a bet.' The orderly paused to laugh. 'Bill hurled him so high that it took a while for him to come back to mother earth. Broke his arm in three places. No one has been stupid enough to make another attempt.'

Shanahan walked up to Bill. Two more stretchered troopers were being angled and strapped onto his broad back. One of the two orderlies with Bill said: 'Best damned packhorse we've got. He's already been up the track twice today. Never complains, although he can be moody and it's best to steer clear then because, boy, he can kick! But he never gets in a bad temper on the job.' He patted Bill. 'He's a real digger, aren't you, Bill mate?'

Shanahan stroked Bill's face before the orderly led the horse back down the track. He had a chilling feeling he would be seeing a lot of this horse for all the wrong reasons.

He quickly learned how right he was. Soon afterwards, at 4.20 am on 19 May, the Turks hit, with more than 10,000 soldiers screaming their love of Allah as they descended into the valley with a band inspiring them with marching songs. Shanahan opted to climb up to Quinn's to be with his men during the enemy assault. He had been in the trench for ten seconds with his head well down when two grenades were lobbed within a metre of him. A trooper fell on one with two doubled-up blankets. He pushed down hard. The explosion a split second later threw the trooper hard into a trench wall. He was stunned but relieved to feel all his body parts and limbs intact.

Shanahan had nothing to smother the second grenade with. It bounced on soft earth and spun like a top in front of him. Instinctively, Shanahan scooped it up and hurled it back at the Turkish trench. It exploded. Judging from the accompanying screams it had hit home.

Quinn's Post was not the only one being hit as the Turks surged down into the face of a powerful defence from Anzac machine-gunners. Brigadier Monash's engineering skills had paid off. He had placed gunners at strategic spots in a rim of trenches at the head of the valley with orders to move forward if at all possible. At first the Turkish deluge of men was not supported by artillery. This allowed Shanahan and other officers to urge their riflemen to climb onto the parapets and mow down the enemy without the fear of shrapnel raining down on them. The pre-dawn light allowed the defenders to see shadowy figures coming at them.

'It became a wild-pig shoot,' Shanahan later wrote to a relative, 'they kept coming and we kept firing. The Turks fell in huge numbers. It was a bit liberating for my men who had not been able to put their heads up in the week they have been here.'

The defence was effective right around the defensive rim. The Anzacs were able to fulfil Monash's wish to set up their weapons forward of the trenches. Thousands of Turks were cut down by 8 am but they kept coming, like tidal waves, from the heights.

The defenders did not have it all their own way. Bill and the other horses and mules were kept busy, especially when the Turks finally got their artillery operating. The Anzac field ambulancemen and animals showed as much courage as any of the combatants operating all around them as they moved about the valley retrieving the fallen. Everyone noticed Bill in particular and his minder, along with a gritty yet always cheery Englishman, John Simpson, and his small donkey. These four did not stop in the first few hours when the crossfire was at its peak. They scurried into no-man's land, loaded up with two injured men and hurried down to dressing stations. Seeing this, the troopers and diggers applauded. This kind of appreciation from the men was repeated many times, with Bill or the donkey being led alternately into the firing zone.

Monash, who witnessed Simpson's selfless, fearless missions, wrote to his wife: 'This man [Simpson] has been working in this [Monash] valley since 26th April in collecting the wounded . . . He had a small donkey, which he used to carry all cases unable to walk. Private Simpson and his little beast earned the admiration of everyone at the upper end of the valley . . . Simpson knew no fear. He moved unconcernedly amid shrapnel and rifle fire, steadily carrying out his self-imposed task day by day.'

But on the day when Monash's defence and a thousand diggers and troopers had shown enormous tenacity in holding back the onslaught, Simpson's luck ran out. At about 9 am it was his turn to take his donkey out in front of Bill and his ambulanceman as they spotted yet another fallen digger. A spray of shrapnel hit him and his animal. Without a second thought, the ambulanceman hustled forward with Bill. Simpson, his body limp, was placed on Bill and hurried away. The Anzacs applauded again, but this time it was muted as they saw the donkey had not moved and Simpson's body was not receiving any urgent attention from the orderlies. This wonderful and inspiring combination of fearless man and beast would no longer come to the aid of hurt comrades.

8

SLAUGHTER AT THE NEK AND QUINN'S

After living through the hell in Monash Valley for the vital early weeks at Gallipoli, Shanahan and his battered regiment were given well-earned garrison duties away from the front line. They were positioned not far from the beach between Anzac Cove and Suvla Bay. Bill the Bastard, too, had earned a break away from the heavy and dangerous work up and down the track to the valley. He was assigned to carry the non-urgent mail in heavy sacks from Suvla Bay to the cove, trotting along beside a mounted trooper at dusk when it was much harder for Turkish snipers to strike them.

*

After a four-month stalemate in which the Turks locked down the Anzacs at Gallipoli and other Allied forces at Cape Helles, in early August 1915 the British generals decided it was time to break out in one mighty coordinated attempt to take the heights. But again, the emphasis was more on using front-line fighters in big numbers in the hope they could do the impossible, *somehow*, rather than devising any great tactical plan that would win and at the same time preserve men.

The prospects for the huge counterattack were not promising for the troopers, who now faced similar experiences to that of Shanahan and his squad in May. Hundreds of Light Horsemen from Western Australia's 10th Regiment and Victoria's 8th, at Russell's Top on the left of Monash Valley facing the heights, would have to charge across a narrow, hemmed-in expanse called the Nek. It was about the size of two tennis courts. A serve from a bank of machine-guns would greet them.

Across at Quinn's seventy metres away, Shanahan and his squadron had returned for this big push. He and the other officers were under orders from Chauvel to send their men north to Baby Hill 700, where the troopers at Russell's Top would also be heading.

The 8th Regiment's troopers at Russell's Top were first over the parapets before dawn. The Turks heard them coming and opened up with 30 machine-guns that created a wall of bullets the width of the Nek. Many men were hit climbing out of the trenches. Some only managed a few paces before being felled. Most were slaughtered when still a tennis court length away from the Turkish trenches. The handful that did reach them was outnumbered by the enemy. The first line of troopers had been cut down in ten minutes.

Shanahan led a select squad out on the order of his brigade commander, along with other officers with similar small bands of troopers. But they, too, were cut down by intense fire from trenches above them. Inside two minutes, fifty of fifty-five troopers were killed. Shanahan, who had dashed out first, was the last man back, protecting the men in front of him as they withdrew. For a third time, he was most fortunate not to have been killed. He slumped into Quinn's. His immediate superior consulted him.

'Any chance of a second wave getting through?' he was asked anxiously.

Shanahan shook his head as he looked around to see how many of his men had made it. That was enough for the officer commanding. He got word to Chauvel, who agreed that this battle was unwinnable.

Troopers waiting to leap out of the trench at Russell's Top did not have such a humane and intelligent command. Their leader, Jack Antill, an Australian who had made his name in Boer War Light Horse charges, had become a shrill and bullying commander at Gallipoli. He ordered a second wave of 150 troopers from the 8th Regiment over the top. After climbing over their fallen cobbers, they too faced the horrors of the Nek and were sliced into by the enemy machine-gunners. Then followed lines three and four, this time from the 10th

Regiment. They suffered the same fate as the Victorians. Within a short time, hundreds of troopers lay dead or wounded in a sweep from Russell's Top to the Turkish trenches. Antill still wanted action but he was over-ridden now by more sensible heads among Australian officers, who appealed to senior commanders. But it was far too late for some of the cream of the fighting men from Western Australia and Victoria.

The emphasis now along the front was on retrieving the wounded in no-man's land. This was nearly impossible given the Turkish defences. Through the day injured men were noticed moving, crawling a few paces here, raising a hand for help there. But no aid could come. The Turkish guns in the narrow corridors of these battles made it futile to send in the ambulancemen, on this occasion without their animals, which could not be brought up steep ravines or along narrow ridges.

Bill was once more seconded to help out in Monash Valley. He trudged up the track from Anzac Cove to join a dozen other horses and mules lined up at the foot of the ridges. Stretcher bearers and medics were forced to wait until night to help the odd wounded trooper who may have lived through the very long day of 7 August 1915. As soon as dusk settled, the first of the injured were stretch-ered down to the head of the valley where Bill and his fellow pack animals waited. They then began their steady treks with the injured to the dressing stations.

A few days later, he was taken back to Suvla Bay to be loaded up once more with the non-urgent mail and despatches. The inability of anyone to stay on him for more than a couple of minutes, and the fact that he could carry far more than any other animal, had so far saved him from a sniper's bullet.

9

SHOOTING THE
MESSENGER

Each day at Gallipoli a rider carrying the more urgent despatches would make the seven-kilometre run from Suvla Bay north of Anzac Cove to British campaign head-quarters at the cove. This was turned into a macabre event. The Turks in the ridges and hills would snipe at the riders. 'It [the mail delivery] had to be done at the gallop,' Chauvel wrote to his wife. 'The rider was fired at from the moment he left the shelter of Lala Baba until he reached the wide communications trench near Anzac. All the Australian Light Horsemen, New Zealand Mounted Riflemen, and the British Yeomanry [cavalry] were tumbling over each other to get the job.'

Most Anzacs, including officers, would watch. Hundreds would place bets on whether the rider and his horse would make it along the track close to the beach. This pervasive, callous gambling operation was in tune with the attitude to life and death at Gallipoli. The 'run' was hazardous. The Turkish snipers waited for this 'sport' each day and would themselves lay bets on who could hit the rider or the horse.

Sergeant Sutherland was running the small remount depot at Suvla Bay. Early in October, he was ordered by General Godley to let an exceptional cavalryman, Captain Anthony Bickworth, mount the most difficult horse in the depot in an attempt to get a despatch through. No one had been shot on this run for two weeks and such was the careless attitude to life and death by this stage on Gallipoli, that the British wanted to change the odds to make it more 'sporting'. In other words, a horseman had to be exceptional to both dodge bullets and keep on his mount. To make it more interesting, Bickworth was assigned to the 'job'. He had the reputation, at least among the British, as the best horseman of the invading troops. But there was another compelling factor. The upper-class Bickworth, the third son of an impoverished landowning British count, had lost a lot of money gambling in Cairo and was deeply in debt. He would be offered an 'incentive' of 100 pounds to risk his skills and life on the despatch run. Bickworth had been at Cape Helles at the peninsula's tip. He was ferried up to Suvla Bay at night.

Anzacs and British soldiers had a meeting. The bet was that either the mail would get through, or it would not. Trooper Swifty Thoms let slip that Bill the Bastard would make it impossible for any rider, no matter who was on him, to make it. Sutherland was then ordered to break out Bill for this 'special' ride. A heavy plunge went on the mail *not* getting through. Thoms and a few mates, including Sutherland, now got odds up to twenty to one from the various bookies at the cove. They were betting the mail *would* get through. General Godley was informed that Bill would make the journey and changed his mind about the outcome of the ride. He slipped his aide-de-camp twenty pounds to put a secret bet on the mail *not* getting through.

At just after 11 am on 3 October, thousands of Anzacs and British soldiers occupied vantage points above Anzac Cove and close to it to watch this 'event'. The officers and many of the men had binoculars. All artillery, machine-gun and rifle fire stopped. The sun was out and there was a clear view of the path to be taken about thirty metres from the shoreline.

Bickworth, a lean, bony-faced man of forty, was in full yeomanry outfit but for a strange German-style helmet when he strode into the remount depot on the beach near Suvla Bay. Horses rather than people were his passion, and he wasn't even prepared to make small talk with Sutherland. He asked for 'Bill the er . . . er . . . Bastard.' The sergeant picked up on his no-nonsense, 'superior' demeanour and without further word left his tent and broke Bill out from a roped-off section at the little inlet of Lala Baba.

Bickworth had a long whip, more like a stockman's than a jockey's. He tapped his boot with it impatiently as

Sutherland tethered the horse and brought two saddlebags of mail and despatches.

'Quite a bit riding on this, Captain,' the sergeant proffered.

Bickworth ignored him. He did two semicircles of Bill, being careful not to stand close to his rear.

'Been fed?' Bickworth asked.

'And watered . . . two hours ago. Wee Bill doesn't need much.'

'It's a long ride at the gallop.'

'This wee horse would outdo a camel.'

'I doubt that.' He stroked Bill's neck. 'Ugly beast . . .'

'I think he's beautiful.'

'Hmm. Mixed breeds like this are never pretty.'

Bickworth patted Bill on his left flank and neck, indicating he was going to mount him, which he did, easily and professionally. He waited. There was no reaction from Bill.

'Can I say, Captain, go easy on him wi' stirrup and whip.'

'If I wished for a lecture on how to handle a horse from you,' Bickworth snapped, 'I would have asked.'

'Of course, Captain,' Sutherland replied, unfazed, and with his usual languid, careless smile added, 'Good luck to you.'

'Luck?' Bickworth said with disdain as he manoeuvred Bill onto the path.

'You'll need a wee bit o' that,' Sutherland chuckled under his breath.

Rider and horse began at a trot, Bickworth getting a feel for his mount and the path's hold. Bill was compliant. No one had attempted to ride him since the unfortunate trooper Gerry Henderson half a year earlier. Perhaps it was the novelty, or maybe it was because Bill liked this particular track, which he had been on a hundred times since arriving, but he seemed oddly content with this high-in-the saddle rider who had made a name for himself in equestrian events at the Olympics.

High above them in the hills, several Turks rushed to put down their late morning drinks or food or cigarettes and wriggle into position with their rifles. They adjusted their sights. The daily sporting shoot was about to commence.

A few kilometres away, thousands of British soldiers and Anzacs began to pay attention. Godley, high in a sheltered position on Walker's Ridge above Anzac Cove, lifted his binoculars. The only weapons fire now was that from the Turks aiming at Bickworth. All other guns were silent. The 'race' for Anzac Cove was on. Shanahan also used binoculars to watch. He well remembered big Bill for his courageous and goliath-like work in Monash Valley. Now there was another dimension to this horse beyond that of a pack animal, albeit the most powerful that he had ever seen.

Bickworth felt a twinge of nerves because of his unfamiliarity with this horse. It was always a thrill for someone of his vast experience to be on such an animal, especially with its daunting reputation. Very soon, he realised his power. Bill built to a gallop. Bullets plopped into the sand beyond them, or pinged onto the rocks to their left as they rode. Bill swerved left, right, left, regardless of where the bullets hit. Bickworth objected, but realised he had no say in the matter. Bill's head was down. Like a rampaging rhinoceros, he could not be stopped in his unpredictable, rhythmless zigzag, charging on as they reached another stretch of the track.

Godley became animated. He was among a brace of British officers whose binoculars were raised. 'I think this fellow will get away with it after all,' Godley cried in excitement. 'Christ, did you see him duck that time? Look! Look!'

Bill careered on at a fast gallop. Bickworth wanted to rein him back but couldn't. He reckoned the horse would have to slow up soon because it was an impossible run at a full gallop. No horse could ever go at such a pace for that long, he thought, but Bill barrelled on, although his zigzag movements became less frequent, even when snipers got very close. At about a quarter of the way there Bill flinched, slowed up and bucked. A surprised Bickworth fought to stay in the saddle, needing all his reserves of riding skills. At two kilometres another disparate volley of sniper-fire whistled close. Bickworth ducked once more, just when Bill flinched a second time and slowed again. This time he bucked with all his tremendous strength. Bickworth was in the act of ducking a third time as bullets flew and the combination of movements unbalanced him. He was thrown five metres over the horse, landing with a crunch on his shoulder and back. The impact caused his helmet to jerk free.

'They've got him at last,' Godley exclaimed, 'by God they have! That was a bloody fine shot!'

Godley was wrong. He had heard the echo of the shot and seen Bickworth catapult out of the saddle.

Bill stopped about twenty metres further on. He was distressed and frothing at the mouth, but instead of circling back to Bickworth, who lay crumpled and unconscious, the horse moved off again, this time at a trot, still in the direction of the Anzac communications trenches. He knew the destination. The firing had stopped. Turkish bets, which centred on the first sniper to stop rider or horse, were already being settled.

A rotund vet, known at the cove as Sir Cumference, was having trouble roping in a distressed Bill when Shanahan reached the beach. He helped the vet remove the saddle-bags of mail.

'He has a wound on his left flank,' the vet said. 'He is bleeding, not badly but it must be dressed.' He pointed to a roped-off area on the beach fifty metres north. It was an animal sick bay. Shanahan held a metre-long pole with an Australian flag on it which he used for training horses. He touched Bill with it, trying to show that he wasn't going to hurt him. Bill snorted. He seemed to be in pain. Shanahan could see a small rivulet of blood bubbling from the horse's left flank. He managed to shepherd him slowly back to the makeshift hospital, talking to him all the way, gradually gaining some calm, which suggested he had gained a little respect from the horse. He tethered Bill, roping his legs so that he couldn't kick. The vet came close with his satchel and examined the wound.

'I can see the bullet's tip,' he said. 'Have to get it out. Not a big problem.'

The vet took out a bottle containing chloral hydrate. 'Help me ease him down after I drench him. He's a big fella, about three-quarters of a ton, I'd reckon. Will take a fair dose to knock him out but we've got to be careful, this stuff is used to kill them. Can you distract him for a moment?'

Shanahan reached into his pocket and gave the horse a licorice sweet. Bill liked it. He nudged Shanahan on the arm, wanting another. Then he nibbled at his pocket. Shanahan gave him another sweet. The vet pushed the bottle into Bill's mouth and half a minute later the drug took effect. Three assistants helped Shanahan ease Bill to the ground. The vet then went to work, using a long tweezers-like instrument to ease the bullet out. The wound was dressed.

'Did you see the run?' Shanahan asked. 'There were two moments when he flinched. I think he was hit twice.'

The vet raised his eyebrows and stroked his considerable second chin, then he waddled around Bill and examined every bit of his hide with a magnifying glass. He found another bullet hole high on his left rump.

'Not much bleeding, just a little moist.'

'Which means?'

'The bullet is deep. Right through his thick hide. And I mean thick.'

He dressed the second wound with a dexterity that belied his plump fingers, and then put his instruments back into his satchel and closed it. 'Nothing to be done. I've seen plenty of those types of holes. Just about all the animals are walking around with them. Much like the men. Thousands of both have shrapnel shards and bits of bullets lodged in their bodies and the medicos can't get 'em out. Most live with them. Some have pain occasionally; others irritation; others nothing.'

Captain Bickworth was unconscious for an hour. He woke up in pain and diagnosed himself with a snapped collarbone. An ambulance crew crept close and hastened to stretcher him to safety. Meanwhile Swifty Thoms and a few mates collected on their bets. The mail did get through, although the rider did not. They had bet on Bill making it.

*

Only about one-third of the horse and mule contingent had survived Gallipoli by early December 1915. Bill was among them. He recovered quickly from his wounds after his near-fatal mail run and he had made one new friend: Shanahan, who visited him in the sick bay and wherever he was after that. He never attempted to ride him but would often walk him along the beach or take him for a swim. There was also the odd licorice sweet. Shanahan would not claim a bond with the horse at Gallipoli, but the respect from Bill seemed to grow, if only slowly.

79

'Do you know much about his background?' Shanahan asked Sutherland.

'No. Many of the Walers were running wild when we rounded them up for service.'

'He's about five years old, right?'

'Hard to say. He is the fittest, strongest animal I have ever come across in the Scottish Highlands, here or in Australia.'

'Say he is five. Think about his background. He probably was wild as a foal. He had no parenting. Then he comes into contact with humans and they try to dominate him; they treat him rough. But he refuses to buckle. His instinct and experience would tell him he is ten times their size and twenty times more powerful. In any test of strength, he wins, but he loses friends.'

'Look, I don't find him so bad. He bit me hard once, but I often wondered if he was just playing and didn't know his own strength.'

'I reckon he just needs a good cobber.'

'Nah, I think he's too mature for that now. He hates riders and that's that.'

Shanahan illuminated to a near-smile, indicating he didn't agree.

*

In mid-December 1915, some 30,000 Anzacs began beating a silent retreat from Gallipoli, leaving 8000 dead. Shanahan and many other troopers took a moment to visit the rough graves dotted around Anzac Cove before departing. Shanahan was among those who wanted to stay and see the fight through, but he had to accept the proposition that it was better to wait to engage the Turks on another day, on another battlefield. It hurt him deeply, especially leaving so many troopers from country Queensland, most of whom he had known over the journey of the last thirty years in various Light Horse formations. He, like all the other members of the Light Horse, had felt disadvantaged without his mount. They all longed to be reunited with them near Cairo, where they would also be joined by a batch of fresh and eager trooper recruits from Australia.

The thrusting, powerfully built Victoria Cross winner, Lieutenant-Colonel L C 'Elsie' Maygar, forty-four, was chosen for the last defence act at Gallipoli. He selected forty volunteers from among the troopers he knew would fight to the death in defence of the evacuation. They would be stationed at Russell's Top, the scene of so much Light Horse destruction four months earlier.

Maygar asked for only two medicos and met Sutherland just before he closed the depot at Suvla Bay and was about to send his surviving mules and horses onto barges bound for the island of Mudros.

'I want two pack . . .' he began as he looked around. 'Ah yes, that's one of them.' He pointed to Bill. 'That huge bugger . . .'

'Can't have him, I'm afraid, he's a wee bit lame,' Sutherland lied, 'but we have two lovely wee donkeys here . . .'

10

BANJO REMOUNTS

Banjo Paterson learned on his return to Sydney that the army was recruiting Light Horsemen and acquiring tens of thousands more horses as quickly as possible. This meant that after the belting at Gallipoli, the Anzacs would be fighting the Turks on a bigger scale in Egypt, Palestine and perhaps further into Arabia as well. Paterson was fifty-one. He had to put his age down to forty-nine to apply for 'remount service'. The next hurdle was a medical examination. Paterson distracted the doctor looking at his deformed arm by saying he was worried he might have a hernia. The doctor examined his groin and found no problem.

'Except for a bout of hypochondria,' Paterson remarked dryly.

'Perhaps it was phantom pain,' the doctor said with a shrug, and passed him fit for service.

Paterson recalled Harry Chauvel's offer and obtained a letter of recommendation from him. It led to Paterson being made a lieutenant in one of the remount divisions being hastily assembled. He was soon promoted to captain and took a transport ship back to the Middle East. Chauvel was pleased with his return. He promoted Paterson to major and put him in charge of the huge, main remount division based at Moascar near the Suez, not far from Port Said. It was about 220 kilometres north-east of Cairo and Paterson at first recoiled from the relative isolation. He liked to socialise and Cairo was good for that. He could fraternise with many women working for the British. He could drink in the clubs and hotels with the generals and others who would give him stories. Moascar would deny him all that except for leave time. He was not going to be a war correspondent but, as Chauvel pointed out, he would have a far greater impact on any conflict in this new role. The breaking, training and preparation of tens of thousands of horses and mules would be one of the most vital roles of the war in the Middle East. 'If we are going to beat the Turks,' he told Paterson, 'fit horses are essential.'

Paterson wrote of his responsibilities as outlined by Chauvel: 'To take over the rough, uncivilised horses from all over the world by the army buyers; to quieten them and condition them and get them ready for being heel-roped; and finally to issue them in such a state of efficiency that a heavily accoutred trooper can get on and off under fire if need be.'

Breaking the horses in and perfecting their patience under stress would be the difference between life and death for every trooper at least once in battle and, in some cases, often. Paterson soon had 800 rider/trainers under his command, along with 45 vets and assistants. Many buck riders, who roamed Australia in the rodeo shows, had joined the mounted infantry after the outbreak of war had put an end to their performance work.

Some horses in the continual intakes were rougher than Bill the Bastard, who was sent to Moascar to join the mobs arriving from everywhere. But Bill, he believed, would never be fully broken in whereas he was confident he could prepare almost all the others coming under his control. Paterson noticed him wandering the depot grounds. He, like Shanahan, had a soft spot for this big chestnut with the independent mind, idiosyncratic ways and capacity for heavy lifting. He was by no means the most difficult animal at the depot: 'I think everybody [horse sellers in several countries] that had an incorrigible brute in his possession must have sold it to the army.' He drew the line at some of what he termed the 'cheaper' variety, noting, with his sardonic juices runing:

Thousands of these Argentinians were sent over. They were an interesting study to the student of horseflesh. They were squat, short legged cobs with big hips and bad shoulders. Their heads were like the painting of Bucephalus, ridden by Alexander the Great. They were probably bred from Bucephalus, as one fails to guess by which intermixture of strains of blood the type was arrived at. It is certainly a fixed type now. They resemble each other so closely that if one lost an Argentinian pony, there was little chance of identifying it among his comrades.

They are worthless, cow-hearted brutes. No-one who used them ever had a good word for them. They have been good horses in the Argentine but none of them were going to the war.

Paterson believed there was no comparison with his light, wiry Walers and he himself rode the best of them. 'I usually only ride horses intended for generals and thus I got the pick of the mounts,' Paterson wrote.

There was another side to this. If he did not like the general from a particular country, or if the man concerned was rude to him, Paterson was not above delivering him a difficult horse. The animal would not be utterly raw. That would have been too obvious and got Paterson into trouble. Instead he would give the offending general a horse that was temperamental or unpredictable. Then if the general concerned was given trouble by the mount, even bucked off, Paterson could always suggest the rider was a poor horseman. Bill was the perfect horse for this kind of subterfuge. He might let a rider on, as he did Captain Bickworth, and give him a false sense of security for even a few kilometres' ride, but then he would live up to his name and send the man flying. Paterson was unlikely to hand Bill over to anyone for battle purposes, though. He could buck harder than any other horse he had ever encountered and this might kill a man. Yet he planned to put him on display at a big show created to make his remount division 'justly celebrated'.

Just before dawn on the morning of Paterson's remount event, Shanahan arrived at the depot to meet Sutherland, who would take him to see Bill. They met at the front entrance where there was a change of a guard of a dozen soldiers. Two machine-guns were being set up. The light of a full moon was giving way to a wide yellow splash on the horizon and the perpetual promise of scorching heat. The depot was alive with hundreds of trainers crisscrossing the fields to various buildings and tents. Kerosene lamps lit the way to a stable past a corral where buckets were carried and troughs filled. Horses that would be performing were being saddled for a run to open up their lungs. Trick ponies were being loosened up and whispered to by their masters, who would already be feeling nervous.

As they entered the stable, a truck was backing up near them to drop straw bales, which fell with a dull thud on the soft sand. The smell inside was familiar to Shanahan, who had been near or in stables for a fair part of his life: a mixed, musty fragrance of urine, horsehair and sweat on horse blankets, along with oats, hay and grain, which emitted their own sweeter aromas.

'We have a better stable for the special neddies,' Sutherland said. 'I call it the Cup Hotel: home for all the Melbourne Cup candidates and other worthies, including your wee cobber.'

They walked past twenty stalls. A thin young Aboriginal trainer was hosing down the horses.

'That's Khartoum,' Sutherland said, pointing to a big black stallion that looked down an imperious extra-long nose at the intruders. 'He's Banjo's favourite. Says he wants to take him back at the end of all this and have him trained for racing. He only lets the "jockeys"—the smaller blokes who have raced in Australia—on him.'

Sutherland took him over to Khartoum.

'Have a look at his forehead,' Sutherland said, pointing out an ugly scar.

'Your pal Bill did that. Khartoum was apparently flirting with Bill's girlfriend Penny. Bill flew at him and bit him hard. Khartoum bled a fair amount. Vets had to work overtime. He had about 100 stitches. Khartoum is a wee bit frightened of your pal now.' He waved at two other horses, Tut 1 and Tut 2.

'Tut 2 is the stallion,' Sutherland said. 'Tut 1 is the gelding.'

'Should have been Tut Zero, shouldn't he?' Shanahan remarked.

'Banjo reckons he will put Khartoum and Tut 2 out to stud if they don't do that well. They are power horses, stayers. Banjo says that if they don't win the Melbourne Cup, they will sire winners.'

They strolled past stalls.

'That's Blackham,' Sutherland said, pointing to a white mare.

The Aborigine, Jackie Mullagh, splashed water near them. Hearing the conversation, he chipped in: 'I've ridden her. We've clocked her up to a mile. Fastest sprinter in the world, at least Banjo says.'

Sutherland introduced Shanahan to Mullagh, saying, 'He's our best jockey, trainer and rider, by far.'

Mullagh grinned.

'It's true,' he said, causing Shanahan to give a hint of a smile.

'I want a really good trainer for my squadron,' he said.

'Don't even think about it,' Sutherland interjected. 'Banjo won't let him go.'

'Hey, I have a say, don't I?' Mullagh said.

Shanahan changed the subject. 'Where did he get these Arabian beauties from?' he asked.

'All I know is that Banjo did a deal with some big-shot Egyptians,' Sutherland replied. 'You'd have to ask him.' He waved his hand at the stalls. 'Banjo has them trained early in the day before the heat saps them.'

'Is he serious about racing them?'

'Yeah. He reckons he can get them all back home. Dunno how. It's against regulations. But you know him, if there is a rule, he reckons it's there to be broken.'

They strolled on.

'That sweet creature is Bill's girl Penny,' Sutherland said, pointing out an ungainly, overweight silver-grey mare. 'She's a packhorse. Some of the trainers think wee Penny is so ugly that they call her "hatful", which I think is "hateful"! I might say "hatful" was a term unknown to me before I heard it here. But I think she's a wee darlin' mount, if ever there was one. Bill agrees wi' me, but from a different perspective.'

Sutherland noticed a flicker of a grin from Shanahan. The sergeant was beginning to realise that this response was the equivalent of a hearty laugh from anyone else. But Sutherland liked this reticence. It meant he was being listened to, which, as an immigrant to Australia of five years, was not often part of his experience.

'He finds wee Penny most attractive indeed.' Sutherland pointed to Bill. 'They are always at it. We will see plenty of foals out of that union, I can tell you.'

They reached Bill. He recognised Shanahan, nodded his head and moved forward. He brought his face down close to Shanahan, who stroked his nose and neck.

'That's more excitement in him than I've seen in the last few days,' Sutherland remarked, 'apart from when he can get at Penny. He doesn't react much to anything. He is a very cool customer. He only goes berserk when someone tries to mount him. Otherwise, he's a sweet lamb. He can get cranky, but they all can. You know, it might be their feet, something not even the best farrier can pick. Until it's fixed they are moody and down. Not much different from us, really.'

Shanahan ran his hand over the bullet wound. He moved around the side of the stall and examined where the second bullet had lodged and stayed deep. There was hardly a mark.

'Why does Banjo keep him in here with the thorough-breds? Can't be taking him home for a Cup ride, can he?'

'No one is really sure. Banjo believes he can find a trainer who can break him completely. No one has, so far. The nearest to "tame" him is Jackie. He has a go every other day. So far he hasn't stayed on half a minute. But he gets on best wi' the horse. They have a vague rapport. Jackie walks him, feeds him, waters him, hoses him, exercises him. He cleans out his stable. But mounting him stretches their friendship too far. Jackie gets chucked off every time. More bruises on him from Bill than a prize fighter gets in a lifetime. But he keeps getting back on.'

'Robert the Bruce,' Shanahan mumbled.

'Aye, laddie, just like him!' Sutherland said, pleased that the Scottish legend was known.

'Can we walk Bill?' Shanahan asked.

They bridled the horse. Shanahan took him by a long rein and they wandered in a field of sand and scrub. Other horses were being exercised in preparation for the big event. They thundered by on a rough track.

'I take them out most days,' Sutherland said.

'Should be every day,' Shanahan advised, 'to get them breathing. It relaxes them.'

Later in the day, Egyptian notables, wandering English celebrities such as author Conan Doyle, and British officers' wives all arrived to see the grand remount depot show. A wooden grandstand had been erected to hold a few hundred VIPs. Big marquees had been set up. Spectators would grow in number to a few thousand by the noon start time, including several troopers with the day off from patrolling the Sinai. They milled around behind wooden barriers that ringed the arena.

Bill the Bastard was advertised as 'the unridable one: See the world's best riders attempt to tame him'. Paterson placed Bill as the last event on the program. He split the buckjumping show-riders and horse-breakers into a four-state squadron competition. This was followed by an 'international horse-back wrestling' competition. In the England versus Australia match, he reported that 'one of my Queenslanders, a big half-caste named Nev Kelly, pulled the English Pommies off their horses like picking apples off a tree'.

Before the final item, Paterson used a megaphone to inform the audience that only two horsemen had ever stayed on Bill for more than two minutes. The record was 'a Captain Bickworth of the British Cavalry' who stayed on him for two minutes and thirteen seconds continuously at Gallipoli. 'A teenage recruit in 1914 at Liverpool is alleged to have stuck up there [on Bill] for about two minutes ten seconds. But that's it, apart from our own number one trainer here, Jackie Mullagh. He has the record for the number of rides on Bill, but he has never stayed on more than 25 seconds.' Paterson was so confident that Bickworth's time would never be bettered that he offered the tempting prize of 50 pounds to any trainer, or anyone in the audience, who could do better. A hundred trainers applied. Paterson chose the five best, in his judgement, for the challenge, including the talented Mullagh.

A saddled Bill was paraded into the arena to huge applause. He was 'escorted', like a prize fighter into a boxing ring, by six trainers. But he didn't look ready for a fight. He didn't prance, perform or kick up a fuss. He seemed passive and perhaps ready for a nice afternoon nap rather than an exhibition of jockey-throwing. The crowd and noise did not appear to perturb him.

The trainers surrounded him as the first horse-breaker, a wiry, gaunt-faced character wearing yellow clown's trousers, ran into the arena, looking for applause. Number 1 was marked on the back of his shirt. He spoke firmly to Bill, who just watched with a phlegmatic look. The man leapt on. Before he could grip the reins, Bill took off. The rider fell to the ground before the horse even attempted to buck. Bill circled the arena and trotted cheekily up to Number 1 as he scrambled to his feet. It seemed he might collide with him, but Bill pulled up short of the rider, leant back and performed his trademark curl of the lip. Number 1 went to mount him again, but Paterson disallowed it. 'Once you're off, Number 1, you're off,' he called into a loudhailer. 'Next!'

The second rider, a totally bald, bull-necked, stocky individual with a handlebar moustache, carried a stock-man's whip. Before Number 2 made a move for the saddle, he lashed Bill on the rump, then his back. Bill turned to face his tormentor. He reared up, front legs high and kicking. The rider backed off. The six trainers moved in and tried to control Bill, but this second rider could not even get a foot in a stirrup. Number 2 motioned to use his whip again but was admonished by Paterson and some of the trainers. He was disqualified. Paterson gave him a public tongue-lashing for his 'abject stupidity!'

The third rider, a bow-legged, thin little man who walked with a heavy limp, was called for. He put his hands up and shook his head. He knew Bill. The horse was upset. There was no point in trying to mount him. It was a case of once broken, twice shy—Number 3 had acquired a severe knee cartilage problem after a twisting fall from Bill on a previous occasion.

'Very wise, Number 3,' Paterson remarked. 'Discretion is the better part of valour.'

The third rider was jeered. Paterson looked sharply to the main source of the noise. 'Okay, troopers,' he said, 'would one of you like to have a go?'

No one volunteered.

'You too are very wise,' Paterson said. 'This horse will hurt you if he doesn't like you. And he heard your comments. You are marked men!'

This brought a roar of applause.

The fourth rider strode into the arena. He was tall and gangling—all elbows and knees and wearing shorts, black socks and Roman sandals. The six trainers steadied Bill and held on as Number 4 climbed gingerly aboard. He held on to Bill's neck as he began a manic dance near the arena fence. He did one complete circle and then bucked. Number 4 was thrown over Bill's head and into the crowd, which parted so that he hit the ground hard. A medic pushed his way through the throng. The man was in pain. His lower leg was broken—bone was sticking through his shin—and his knee seemed dislocated. Number 4 was stretchered to an ambulance. Paterson thought of calling off the event, but the crowd reacted. They wanted to see Number 5, Mullagh, make his attempt.

The horse was in a fearsome mood now. Mullagh knew he was on a hiding to nowhere. He asked the trainers to remove the saddle, and jumped on. The crowd, which was estimated to have been at more than 5000 by the time of this last event, applauded, whistled and cheered their approval. Bill reared up and stayed high like a trick pony. Mullagh hung on. Then Bill took two paces forward and bucked, his hindquarters lifting so high that it brought gasps from the onlookers. Bill then tilted sideways and Mullagh was off. He had lasted fifteen seconds, which wasn't his best effort.

The multiple leg injuries to Number 4 added to the show's downside. Paterson wrote to a friend that the entire day's performance left him with two men with broken legs, one with a fractured shoulderblade, two with crushed ankles and 'about seven others more or less disabled'. 'Of course Bill the Bastard didn't let me down,' he added with his usual acerbic wit, 'put on a terrifying show. I knew he would add to the casualty numbers. Does every time.' Nevertheless he praised his riders, saying he never had to tell one of them twice to mount a horse, 'no matter how hostile it appeared'. The exception to this concerned Bill. 'We had 100 applications to ride him, but there were 700 that weren't game.'

11

THE WHISPERING LESSON

Cath Phelan, the vet who had snubbed Paterson on his first trip from Australia, was at the party after the remount depot show. She stood out with her white dress and red broad-brimmed hat, belt and shoes. Paterson had offered her a job at the depot and she was there to discuss it with him. He fussed about her, making sure she was supplied with selective introductions to VIPs and endless champagne. Phelan still treated him with barely contained disdain, but he endured her attitude in the hope that she would accept his work offer.

While she and the other VIP guests were feted with drinks and food, Michael Shanahan sought out Mullagh at the stables.

'I want you with my squadron.'

'Better speak with Banjo,' Mullagh said, rubbing a bruise on his arm after his earlier encounter with Bill.

Paterson was supervising a clean-up when Shanahan strolled over to him. 'Major, could I have a little session with Bill?' he asked.

Paterson was unsure. 'He's had a rough day. All that bucking and jumping takes a lot out of him.'

'I don't want to ride him, just get acquainted again.'

Paterson was bemused. 'I won't give him to you as a permanent mount, Lieutenant, for your own sake. You saw him today.'

'He was in good form.'

'Think you can break him, do you?'

'I don't want to break him.'

'He won't bend to anyone's will.'

'I know.'

Paterson considered the lieutenant. 'Like him, do you?'

'Most interesting horse I've ever met.'

'Why so?'

'He has a wonderful spirit. There's an unusual intelligent streak in him.'

'He's very angry about something!'

'Aren't we all, Major?'

They both smiled.

'But you can have any number of the wild ones . . .' Paterson said.

'I saw them today—raw, spirited and unruly. Good stallions and mares among them. But Bill is only a bastard when he chooses. He usually lets riders up on him. Then he decides when they come down.'

'Right enough,' Paterson agreed. He signalled to a trainer for Bill to be brought to them. 'You've got an hour. After that it's bedtime for him and the rest of them.'

Bill was irritable at this extra session with a human. It seemed he had had enough excitement for one day. But he remembered Shanahan so well, it appeared, that he also recalled the left pocket of his trousers where the licorice sweets once were. He nudged it. Shanahan laughed. He had none on his person. He heel-roped Bill, who kicked a little. It was late. He was hungry and thirsty, and tired.

Shanahan had his Australian flag on a pole. He tapped Bill with it. Bill flinched at first, clearly expecting the kind of whip that had been used by one of his would-be 'conquerors' an hour earlier. Soon he was accustomed to the feather slap of the flag. Shanahan manoeuvred him this way and that, using the flag to waft around him or onto his tail-end to ensure movement in a certain direction. Bill snorted in protest but when Shanahan pulled gently on the reins, the horse responded and stopped jerking his head. Shanahan had him doing a left, right, stepping action, like the beginning of dressage training. Bill didn't object. He played the game. He was worked back and forth, then around the yard. The next move was backwards. Bill took several minutes to get used to it, but again he obliged.

Most of the guests at the party, along with about 200 depot employees, had filtered outside to the arena to watch this exhibition in training. Paterson was displeased that the Shanahan–Bill 'show' had disrupted the convivial flow of the celebration. The chatter had given way to almost silent fascination. Paterson looked at his watch.

'He's been at it forty-five minutes,' he said to Sutherland, 'another fifteen and that's it.'

'I've never seen any of the trainers work like this,' Sutherland said. 'He's got Bill almost doing tricks.'

'Pity he'll kick him off anyway.'

'I'm not so sure.'

A quarter of an hour passed.

'Better wrap it up,' Paterson said, 'it's almost dark.'

Sutherland moved towards the fence.

'Wait,' Paterson said. They both paused.

Shanahan was patting the horse's side. He put his arm around Bill's neck and left it there for several seconds. He put his left foot in the stirrup and lifted himself up parallel with the horse without throwing his right leg over.

'We're going to do this,' Shanahan said matter-of-factly, 'Okay, mate?'

Bill stood stock still, as if in a trance. Shanahan mounted him. He patted Bill's neck. Bill pawed the ground, but not aggressively. It was almost like a caress. Neither Paterson nor Sutherland had seen the horse do this. Shanahan nudged him with his heel. Bill moved forward. He was walked around the inside of the fence, ever so slowly building to a trot. Next Shanahan began to manoeuvre him, left, then right. Finally he edged him backwards.

'Amazing!' Sutherland exclaimed.

'Just tricks,' Paterson said. 'The real "trick" would be at a full gallop.'

'You're right. But I've never seen anyone work him like that.'

Shanahan finished his training and dismounted in near darkness to spontaneous applause from the hundreds of intrigued depot staff and guests who had watched most of the session. He tethered Bill, walked to his bag and pulled out some licorice sweets.

'Not a reward,' Shanahan said as he let the horse gobble two pieces from his hand, 'just a thank you.'

He was walking out of the camp to be driven to Cairo for a few days' leave when Phelan hurried past military guards towards him.

'Michael,' she said, 'I watched you with that mighty stallion. Quite a miracle!'

They shook hands. In high heels, she was just taller than Shanahan. He continued walking. Phelan, and her strong perfume, kept pace with him.

'Here for the show?' he asked.

'Yes. Banjo invited me. He wants me to work as a vet here.'

'And will you?'

'No. It's too isolated for me. Cairo is lively. If I have to be in Egypt, that'll do. My fiancé is based there. He's a diplomat liaising with the British High Command.'

They stopped walking. Shanahan waved to his mates, sergeants Mulherin and Legg, who were sitting in a small truck.

'That's my ride,' he said, hoisting his kit on his shoulder.

'I've got my car. Would you like a lift?'

'I . . .' Shanahan began hesitantly.

'I'd love the company,' she said, touching his arm. She glanced at the truck. 'I'm staying at the Savoy,' she said. 'Your friends can meet you there.'

'Why not?' Shanahan said. He sauntered over to the truck.

'My, you're working well,' Mulherin said.

'Jeez!' Legg remarked, 'I saw her in the crowd. What a looker! And what a body!'

'Settle down, fellas. She's engaged. She has offered me a lift to Cairo. We can meet at the Greek cafe.'

Mulherin and Legg looked at each other and laughed.

'We'll see you for breakfast tomorrow at our hotel,' Mulherin said.

'Better make it coffee in the cafe, late tomorrow morning,' Legg remarked with a knowing grin.

'I'll meet you jokers at the Greek place tonight as planned,' Shanahan said.

Shanahan joined Cath Phelan and they walked to her car, a sable-coloured Rolls Royce.

'Nice car,' he remarked. 'How do you get this?'

'Oh Bob—my fiancé—is well connected. There are plenty of officers running around in them. It's on loan from the British army.'

'Nice loan.'

'I told him I'd move to London or Paris for the rest of the war. Bob got it for me to keep me from getting bored.' She laughed. 'But I am still bored.'

Shanahan noticed three dolls sitting in the back seat like silent children.

'Oh, he got me them too,' she said when she saw him looking at them.

'He bought you dolls?'

'I collect them. He knows I love them.'

They drove on in silence for a few kilometres. A goat herder slowed them to a stop as he shepherded his animals across the dirt road.

'You used to box,' Phelan said.

'Amateur. How did you know?'

'You won some championship or other?' she asked, ignoring his question.

'A couple.'

'My father used to box. Said you were the best in the state. You didn't ever lose, if I recall.'

Shanahan didn't respond. Phelan was finding it heavy going. She persisted: 'What made you volunteer?'

'I'd been in the infantry and Light Horse for nearly thirty years. So many of my mates were going in . . .'

'But you're not that young.'

'No,' he said, smiling genuinely for the first time. 'I'll be forty-six soon.'

'When?'

'March thirty.'

'That's tomorrow! Is that why you're going into Cairo? To celebrate?'

Shanahan shrugged. 'My cobbers talked me into it.'

'You should have fun—you don't know when . . .'

He glanced at her.

'Shouldn't have said that,' she said. 'You were lucky to survive Gallipoli.'

'Plenty didn't,' he said softly.

She was distracted by an army truck rumbling behind them. It flashed its lights.

'Let 'em by,' Shanahan said, looking back.

'No, bugger them!' Phelan built up speed. Dust enveloped the car, making visibility poor, but she continued to accelerate. They were soon well clear. Phelan kept up the speed.

'Might as well get there in time for dinner . . . and champagne!'

Shanahan didn't react.

'C'mon, you've got to celebrate with champagne,' she urged. 'Cairo's swimming in it!'

'Don't drink.'

'What, never? Even on your birthday?'

Shanahan didn't respond. Phelan went to say something but checked herself. There was another long lull as the Rolls purred on its way. Shanahan slumped in his seat and pushed his slouch hat over his face. He was soon snoring. After an hour he sat up, blinked and said: 'Sorry. Been a long day. Needed a catnap.'

She pointed to the left. 'See those dark shapes?'

'Pyramids,' Shanahan said, suddenly animated. 'Love them, fascinating.'

'How were they built and who built them, do you think? Were they astronomic observatories? Places of cult worship?'

'Visitors from outer space built them.'

'You believe that?'

'More fun if they did.'

She laughed. Perhaps there was humour embedded somewhere, she thought. Or maybe his every utterance was serious.

'You didn't really say why you volunteered,' she prompted.

He remained silent so long she wondered if she was being ignored.

'It wasn't one thing,' he said finally. 'A few issues flowed together. I wasn't getting any younger. I'm a carpenter, among other things. Never going to earn enough to travel.' He brightened, adding, 'Not to see the pyramids and all this beautiful sand.'

Phelan laughed. 'So, travel . . .' she pressed.

'It was a part of it. Like I said, some mates were going. I had all that training, and it wasn't going to be a pissy little show.'

'Like the Boer War?'

'Right.'

'You wanted to help save the Empire?'

He shrugged and replied: 'I believe in what Brigadier Monash said. He is the most brilliant commander in our entire Anzac force. He gave a lecture at Anzac Cove. His parents were German Jews. He's been to Germany. He reckoned it boiled down to the world accepting military dictatorship or democracy. If the Germans win, they will destroy democracy everywhere. Monash says British dominions will become German colonies. They will want our mineral wealth. That's why we must be here, must contribute, must fight.'

This loquacious outburst was even more encouraging for Cath Phelan. There was something working very well inside that handsome head, she thought. After watching him handle Bill so patiently, skilfully and thoughtfully, she felt he also had to have something different in his make-up, something admirable; perhaps, at least, something compassionate.

They arrived at the Savoy at 9.30 pm. A military policeman parked the car. Phelan asked Shanahan to join her for dinner.

'No, thank you,' he said.

'Going to meet your friends?'

'I did promise them.'

'Will you be in Cairo again soon?'

'In a week. Got more leave. Going to have another crack at Bill at Moascar and then come here for two nights.'

'Could we have dinner then?'

He considered her, making rare eye contact, and said: 'Yeah, why not? It would be good.'

They shook hands. Phelan kissed him on the cheek. Shanahan moved off into the humid Cairo night.

12

A TERM OF ENDEARMENT

There was more than just genuine affection in Shanahan's mind in his reacquaintance with Bill. Like all the troopers, he wanted the best horse possible for what lay ahead: battles in the desert under the most trying conditions imaginable. The Walers were doing well but they had not been tested in the heat of conflict, nor had they been extended on the sort of rides—sometimes seventy to eighty kilometres in a day—they would be required to do in the dry, hot desert. The contention from everyone in the British command was that the camels would always be a better bet on the long marches. They could go days with little or no water. They had been bred in the desert for thousands of years. The Walers had been bred into semi-desert or arid regions of Australia for barely a century. Yet with all that, almost all troopers opted for the Light Horse regiments rather than the camel units. The reason was simple. The troopers to a man wanted to experience the *charge*. They could do this on camels but not at the same speed or with the same chance of success. The Arabs used camels to charge at the Turks or at each other in tribal wars, but there were rarely more than fifty in an attack, and usually it was in an ambush. The Anzac commanders and troopers had visions of attacks by several regiments— up to 1000 horsemen—in mighty onslaughts that would overwhelm the enemy and win major battles.

Shanahan saw the huge potential in Bill and his bastardry. His courage was evident in all circumstances. He was afraid of no man and no man was his master. His reaction when fired on and hit twice on the despatch run at Gallipoli had demonstrated a *will* to ride on even though disabled. He was also stronger than any other of the 200,000 animals that would pass through the British horse depots on the Western Front and in the Middle East. He had been loaded with more than 400 kilograms and it made little difference to his capacity to plough his way along a track, up a gully, or down a ravine. Endurance was a further asset. He also had remarkable speed over long distances. His seven-kilometre gallop was recorded as the fastest time by any horse in eight months of 'runs', and this was despite being hit and interrupted by his desire to remove his rider. Admittedly, he did not have the 80-kilogram Captain Bickworth for much more than a mile (1600 metres). But Swifty Thoms clocked his first

3200 metres (two miles) at just under four minutes, which he reckoned was 'bloody good' considering he was carrying a bigger than average man on his back for about half that distance before he 'shed him like a lizard's skin'. 'The Bastard wouldn't win a Melbourne Cup,' Thoms added, 'but he'd give any horse alive a run for his money over twice that distance [four miles].'

Spirit, intelligence, durability and strength—these factors drew Shanahan to the horse. He and thousands of troopers like him did not have to reflect on the value of a proficient animal to their existence in Australia. It was a given. They were essential for survival in the bush. They were still the main means of travel, despite the development of trains and automobiles. In the even harsher climate of the Middle East, and in battle conditions, they were even more valuable.

*

Without access to intelligence coming into the British Cairo spy centre known as the 'Arab Bureau', Shanahan and his men were sure the Turks would be coming at the British forces across the Sinai. The Turks had been victorious at Gallipoli. In March 1916 they had defeated the British again in Iraq in a battle over its central province. The Ottoman (Turkish) Empire may have been on the wane in Europe, but its leaders were determined to hold on to its 400-year dominance of the Middle East. The Turks were confident, even justifiably cocky, after drubbing the British Empire twice. They were not going to stop. Egypt, which was controlled by the British, was now in their sights. Like the troopers in the field, most observers, including the British spies at the Arab Bureau, believed it was only a matter of time before they sent a big army into the Sinai. The Turkish aim would be to smash its opposing empire for a third successive time, perhaps inside a year.

Every trooper, from Harry Chauvel down to the lowliest private, wanted revenge against the Turks, but it wasn't something spoken with vehemence around camp-fires at night. Any chat in relation to Gallipoli consisted of grumbles about 'not finishing the job', or the fact that so many mates had been left in makeshift graves when the rest evacuated. There were always complaints about the officers, but more vitriol and resentment were directed at the British generals and government for the folly of attacking Turkey with such a poor plan in the first place. Yet unspoken was the feeling that the regrouped Anzac force, which had licked its wounds and re-energised, would like to lash out against the enemy in an effort to at least square the battle ledger. They believed they would acquit themselves far better with what they saw as their major asset in any conflict: their mounts. Yet belief was one thing, reality another. The Walers had yet to be tested under battle conditions in this conflict. Although there was some indication of potential success from their efforts in the Boer War, South Africa was not a desert country.

A problem for the British High Command was judging when a mass Turkish attack on Egypt would occur. The enemy would take their time with this, refitting and rebuilding their own victorious forces. They were not willing to use the three armies already stationed in the Middle East, one in Palestine, another in Jordan, and a third stationed along the Hejaz railway, which ran from northern Palestine to deep into Arabia. The Turks and their German alliance commanders were nervous about shifting these forces south and east just yet. Better, they thought, to rebuild the army that had defended Gallipoli so well and send it on the mission to take Egypt. The Germans and Turks were not going to pass on the chance to knock the British out of the Middle East forever, but they did not wish to make the same mistakes the British had in invading Gallipoli. They would be well-equipped and prepared for protracted battles.

The Turkish delay in sending a force into Egypt in 1916 was not a tactical move, but it had the effect of destabilising the British forces as they waited impatiently for battle. The interlude caused a dangerous lull in defensive thinking. Some of the British forces became slack, which made them vulnerable to sporadic attacks by Turkish patrols seeping stealthily into the Sinai from Palestine where the two enemy armies were based.

*

Shanahan visited the Moascar depot a week after the rodeo show and asked for Bill again. It was late afternoon. He went through the same routine and build-up for half an hour before mounting the horse a second time. Paterson joined Sutherland to watch once more from just outside their 'office' tent.

'He has asked to take him on a ride,' Sutherland said.

'Hmm. I want to see this.'

A trainer, one of a hundred who had been in the yard watching Shanahan exercising Bill, opened the gate and Bill trotted out. Shanahan built him slowly to a gallop. Paterson and Sutherland rushed in to retrieve their binoculars. They hurried to the depot entrance with the group of trainers, who also watched, almost in silence.

Shanahan pushed Bill to a fair clip without letting him do his headlong charge that had ended badly for Captain Bickworth and painfully for trooper Henderson. About 700 metres into the ride, Bill slowed down himself. Shanahan knew this was the precursor to an attempt to unseat him. Bill did as expected with an upward thrust of his rump and back legs. Shanahan braced without losing control. It seemed nothing like the force Bill had generated with the rodeo riders or Bickworth. Shanahan waited for a second buck and it came with a fraction more vigour, but again, from atop the horse it seemed nothing like his previous displays. Then came a third and fourth 'jump' that seemed more playful than an angry attempt to throw him off. Shanahan patted the horse's neck and he settled into a steady gallop again in a circle of about two kilometres into the desert and then back to the depot.

He trotted into the grounds where hundreds of trainers and depot employees had gathered. They applauded.

In their business a wild one like Bill was the ultimate conquest.

Paterson reached up and shook Shanahan's hand. 'Wonders never cease,' he said. 'Never thought I'd see Bill so compliant.'

'Still needs work,' Shanahan commented, 'but I reckon he'll be ready for service in a couple of weeks.'

'You've tamed the bastard.' Paterson grinned and added, 'You even got me turning his name into a term of endearment—almost! Never thought I'd say that after he bit a piece out of Khartoum's head!'

'Then I can take him? I'd be honoured.'

'No, you can't.' A sly smile creased Paterson's rugged features. 'Unless you can arrange a dinner for me with the magnificent Cath Phelan—the woman you left with last time.'

'You haven't tried asking her yourself?'

'Oh yes I have. But she sort of deflects the request.'

Shanahan eyed Paterson for several seconds. 'Can't do that, sorry,' he said.

'Pity. No dinner, no horse.'

'It is a pity, really,' Shanahan said as he dismounted. 'More than you know.'

'Why?' Banjo asked, intrigued.

'She likes you. Loves your ballads. We discussed you on the ride to Cairo.' Shanahan paused and added, 'I'm sure you'll come up again tonight over dinner.'

'You serious, Major? She has never even mentioned my writing to me.'

'She can recite every verse of "The Man From Snowy River".'

'She hardly said a word to me at the party last week!'

'Despite appearances, she's quite shy. Needs a few drinks to get her talking.'

Normally Shanahan was not big on eye contact unless reprimanding one of his squadron troopers, but now he studied Paterson's every twitch as if reading him. 'Tell you what I'll do,' he said in a generous tone, 'if you let me have young Jackie Mullagh *and* Bill, I'll arrange that dinner with Cath. And it will be on me.'

'You are joking! He's our best trainer!'

'Only want to second him for six months, to help my squadron's mounts get right up to standard.'

'Three months.'

'Five.'

'Done,' said Paterson, grinning.

Bill was taken to his corral, but he suddenly broke free from the trainer and trotted up behind Shanahan.

'Look out, Lieutenant,' Sutherland called, 'you've got company!'

Shanahan turned slowly to face Bill and stood his ground. The horse stopped close to him and nudged his shoulder, firmly but without aggression.

'Aha!' Shanahan said. 'You want a reward.' The horse nudged him again. Shanahan reached down to his backpack and pulled out several licorice sweets.

'I guess it might be a reward this time,' he said as Bill devoured the sweets, 'you big bloody kid!'

The prim Savoy waiter poured the champagne into Cath Phelan's glass and walked away. The dining room, dominated by white walls, ceiling and tablecloths, was crowded with British officers and a few Australians. Phelan, in a black dress with a white-brimmed hat and matching white shoes and handbag, was one of four women in the room, and the best dressed. Many heads had turned when she and Shanahan walked in and when they were seated. Several men kept glancing at her.

'You are very popular,' Shanahan observed.

'Ah well, you get used to it here. European, upright, breathing and female.' She smiled. 'I qualify on all counts. Oh, and I'm more than six feet in high heels.'

'And you wear that perfume . . .'

'You like it?' Phelan asked with wide grin.

'It's . . .' Shanahan groped for a description.

'You don't like it?'

Shanahan shrugged. 'Didn't say that,' he said cautiously. 'I will say my olfactories have been alerted.'

'Well I love it! It's French. Bob got it for me in Paris: "La Passionata". He loves it. It may be a bit powerful for you.'

'But not for Banjo Paterson.'

Phelan frowned. 'What?'

'He is very keen on you.'

'Is he? He's a nice man. A very talented, interesting man.'

She clinked her glass with his. Shanahan had water.

'So,' she said eagerly, 'how did it go? Have you won "the Bastard"?'

'It went well. Rode him out for a mile or so. No problem.'

'Great!' She raised her glass again. 'To Bill the Bastard!' It was loud enough for more heads to turn. 'So Banjo has let him go to you?'

Shanahan pulled a face. 'Bit of a problem there,' he said. 'I can have him on one condition.'

'What?'

'That I arrange a dinner between you and Banjo.'

Phelan laughed. 'You bloody men have a cheek! Trading me, not *like* horseflesh, but *for* horseflesh!'

'Will you do it for me?'

'What does he expect?' she asked pointedly.

'Nothing! Just to have dinner with you, that's all.'

She considered him. After a few seconds she said: 'I'll do it with my own condition.'

'Anything!'

'That you'll sleep with me.'

Shanahan blinked and then stared.

'Ah, got some real emotion out of you,' she said.

'Will you dine with Banjo, please?' he asked.

Phelan sipped her drink. 'Why not?' she said phlegmatically. 'I don't fancy him. Just as long as he takes me to dinner somewhere really nice.'

'I appreciate this. We'll put Bill on the train for Romani in a couple of days. Still plenty of work to do. Not that much time. There is a rumour that the Turks are preparing to attack us in the Sinai. I look forward to a good relationship with him in the field.'

116

Phelan drained her glass and motioned for a waiter to refill it.

'You like your champagne,' Shanahan observed.

'I had a couple in the lounge before you arrived too.' She took another sip. 'In the blood, really. My dad was an alcoholic.' She stared at him. 'Don't know how you avoid it.'

'Never had the desire.'

She took a cigar from her handbag and fitted it in the gold holder. She handed him an embossed silver lighter and motioned for him to light it for her. He obliged.

'I suppose you don't smoke either?' she said, offering him one. He shook his head.

'Your dad Tom used to drink at the Roma Hotel with my dad. They were both drunks.' She waited for a reaction. Shanahan was looking at the menu.

'What are you having?' she asked.

'The lamb chops.'

'Me too. There's an English cook. They'll be good.'

She smoked for a while and sipped her champagne before asking: 'Old Tom was tough on you, wasn't he?'

'We all copped a fair bit of abuse, physical and mental. But there were a lot of us, remember—a lot of brats to keep in line. I was the first-born male. I guess Dad made all his mistakes as a parent on me.'

'I remember being at your place and someone broke a window. There were about twenty kids playing cricket. No one owned up to it, so he lined us all up and belted us round the legs with a garden hose!'

The remark teased a hint of a smile from Shanahan. 'Very democratic of him,' he said.

'But my sisters and I had nothing to do with it! He still dished it out and we weren't even his kids!' The shock seemed to revisit her.

'Scarred for life, are we?' Shanahan asked.

'No, of course not. I just remember it. I also saw him strapping one of your brothers to a kitchen chair and belting him with a scrubbing brush.'

'If it was Joe,' Shanahan said with a wry look, 'he probably deserved it.'

'You're defending your father, aren't you?'

Shanahan didn't respond.

'I remember you were the father figure for your younger siblings,' she went on, 'you protected them from old Tom.'

'"Protected" is too strong. My older sister Polly and I used to look after them. Best to keep them away from Dad if he was drunk, which was every night. But he worked bloody hard, you know.'

'Never any excuse. Your father was a moody, heavy-handed bully like mine.'

'He could be melancholic.'

'Don't give me the "poor maudlin Irish" excuse, please.'

'I think you're overstating things.'

'Bullshit!'

Her loud swearing caused the room to fall silent. She drank more. A waiter took their orders. 'And more champagne,' Phelan said as the waiter collected the menus.

She finished her cigar. 'It's the reason I'm thirty-four, not married and haven't had children.'

'Pardon me?'

'All that drinking by Dad, night after night. He would come home and verbally abuse my mother. She would argue back. He'd hit her, not every night, but sometimes. That was bad enough. We used to cop abuse too. I swore I'd never marry. I haven't. But I'm engaged.' She held up her ring finger. 'Yet it's only for show. Saves Bob a bit of embarrassment over "living in sin". He can always say we are getting married next year or when the war's over. But he knows how I feel.'

She lit a second cigar herself. They sat in silence. Shanahan seemed relaxed despite her probing, which she thought might have upset him.

'You used to be an equestrian,' he said, suddenly recalling her. 'You were about thirteen.' He brightened. 'You were really good!'

'That wasn't a question, was it?'

'No . . .'

'Just wondered. Don't think you've asked me one thing since we met.'

A fresh bottle of champagne was popped and poured.

'To answer your non-question,' she said, 'yes, I did have a go as an equestrian. But when we had to move to Brisbane it became too costly to have me indulged. Horses are an expensive business and I had five siblings who needed their own less costly indulgences. Like tennis and cricket. But I have always loved horses.' She held his

119

gaze. 'You do understand why we love them so much?' she said.

Shanahan waited. He knew she would tell him.

'You can relate to them. You find it much easier than humans. And they are loyal. They don't let you down, abuse you or leave you. You learn that if you treat them well and with respect.'

Shanahan nodded almost imperceptibly.

'Don't tell me you haven't realised that,' she persisted. 'That's the reason, or let's say a *big* reason, you can handle Bill the Bloody Bastard when nobody else can.'

Their meals were served.

'Are you married, Michael?' she asked as she added some Worcestershire sauce to her chops and mashed potatoes.

He sampled a chop.

'You do ask a lot of questions,' he said pleasantly. 'Tell me about your fiancé.'

She reached across the table and placed her hand on his.

'Are you going to sleep with me?' she asked.

13

SHADOWS IN
THE DESERT

Shanahan's regiment was warned by a Light Horse
outpost: German planes were in the area and coming
towards his HQ encampment in the Sinai twenty kilometres from the coast. He raised the alarm, causing a hundred
troopers to scurry to their horses and gallop straight into
the desert. Shanahan was nervous. This was the first real
test for Bill. He had come through several practice runs of
this kind, but how would he perform facing a real threat?
If he reverted to his former capricious nature he could be
trouble. What if he bolted and became a target?

Shanahan galloped off just as the other troopers spread
out in all directions for several hundred metres. He could
just hear the steady drone of a German biplane buzzing in
the cloudless sky. Shanahan pulled Bill up close to some

scrub, patted him and said: 'Okay, we stop here for a few minutes, cobber.'

After the hectic scatter of minutes earlier, there was hardly a movement. Shanahan could see horses and riders frozen in positions near scrub and palm trees in every direction. From ground level it seemed impossible that they would not be sighted from the plane, but experience had taught the troopers that pilots and their observers could not differentiate between the Light Horse and the vegetation.

The German plane appeared, at first just a dot on the horizon. The drone grew louder. Shanahan looked up. He felt nervous and a little helpless. There was nothing to fight back with if the plane dropped its bomb. He cared not for himself but for his men, whom he had drilled well. He assured them they would not be struck if they stayed motionless, but this was a crucial moment. Would the theory be proved correct? The plane circled, which indicated the Germans had intelligence that there were troopers in the area. Then the plane wobbled low.

'Jesus,' Shanahan whispered. He could make out the hooded heads of the pilot and observer as they looked this way and that, trying to spot any prospective target. The plane swooped so low that it seemed it might land, which could have been a fatal move. The soft sand would make take-off difficult. But the Germans were not going to come down. They were skimming the dunes to find their hidden quarry. After about twenty minutes of circling and lowering with the incessant fearsome drone splitting the silent desert air, the Germans flew off north and back to a base just over the border in Palestine, a mission unfulfilled.

Shanahan trotted back to his tent at a small oasis. He was satisfied that he could trust his horse on an important manoeuvre. He was also relieved that none of his men had been hit.

He and his squadron still had to wait for action. There were daily grumbles but just one trooper deserted. Shanahan took this down-time to work his horses up to peak condition, using Jackie Mullagh as the top trainer. In return, Mullagh asked for special training sessions with Bill. He claimed to have been tipped off 30 times, but he would not give up. He was resilient and determined. Shanahan obliged. He walked Bill and Mullagh out to a scrubby area near their oasis HQ.

'Horses have an instinct for rhythm and movement,' he told Mullagh as he walked Bill around in much the same manner as he had after Paterson's exhibition. 'You got to work them up to it by repetitive movements. Think of him as a natural dancer.'

Shanahan asked Mullagh to mount Bill.

Mullagh got on gingerly, expecting to be bucked off at any second. But Shanahan kept walking him up and back, around and backwards. Bill eased into the rhythm, almost as if he was unaware of his rider.

Shanahan counted: 'One, two, three. One, two, three . . .'

Bill was prancing to the numbers. After ten minutes of this routine, Shanahan pulled Bill up. He patted him, and told him how good he was.

'Now dismount,' Shanahan said.

Mullagh slid off and stood back, again expecting to see the horse's powerful hind legs kick. But they did not. Shanahan positioned Mullagh next to him and held the reins with him. He built into a slightly different rhythm. Under his breath he said: 'Now you hold the reins. I'm pretending to hold them.' Shanahan inched away, leaving Mullagh in charge. When a further ten minutes elapsed, Shanahan called a halt.

'You don't want me to mount him again?' Mullagh asked, surprised.

'No. You haven't got his respect yet. That will take time.'

They strolled Bill back to squadron HQ.

'You have to wheedle him,' Shanahan said.

'Huh?'

'Cajole him, charm him. You have to bend him to your will without the bend, if you get my drift.'

'Bribe him?'

'No, never.'

'But I seen you give him them licorice sweets.'

'If you watch closely, I never give them as a reward. I stroke and pat him, even give him a hug sometimes. That's his reward.'

'I think I get it.'

'You gotta be strict but fair.'

Each day they went through a similar routine for half an hour. After ten days Shanahan surprised Mullagh by asking him to take Bill for a ride. All seemed to go well. Shanahan got on another horse and trotted after them. When he was near, Bill suddenly stopped and hurled Mullagh to the ground.

'Why the hell did he do that?' Mullagh asked, brushing sand from his body. He was shaken. 'It was goin' so smooth!'

'Maybe he got bored. Who knows with Bill? But you both did okay. You were up there for more than two minutes.'

The days dragged by. The sun was strong. Some Anzacs had sunstroke during blistering days. Many of the troopers had come from hot, semi-arid regions of the north and west, but they had never encountered regular temperatures of 45 to 50 degrees Centigrade. Rifle bolts scalded hands and boots shrank. The heat had a constant companion of swirling winds which sometimes created sandstorms that bit and burned exposed skin. The sand itself became an enemy cursed more than the Turks. The winds carried uncomfortable whiffs of the desert, where the stench of decaying bodies—humans, horses and camels—lingered in the scattered and sporadic desert war. Birds of prey circled and caught the attention of troopers but not nearly as much as the flies, which irritated them as they had at Gallipoli.

The impatient troopers were finding plenty to complain about as they waited for action. The sustained diet of bully beef and rock-hard biscuits was not helping although there were promises from the High Command that it would be improved. Water was restricted to one bottle of a few litres every twenty-four hours. It was not enough, and troopers were often caught using water from the horse troughs to refill their containers. Their ration was often brackish and not made more palatable by chlorine tablets, which the army doctors made compulsory. The dissolved chlorine was supposed to kill bacteria. The troopers used it for cleaning the rust off stirrup irons.

There was the odd skirmish or distant encounter with Turkish patrols drifting down from Palestine to test the Light Horse and cavalry strength and resolve, but apart from these adrenalin rushes, there had been nearly four months of relative inaction in 1916. More troopers considered deserting and catching a boat to Europe to join the Allied forces fighting the Germans.

*

On the night of 23 April 1916, two days short of a year after the first Anzac landing at Gallipoli, Shanahan received an urgent call from Harry Chauvel to ride with a squadron of 128 troopers to Oghratina, a village forty kilometres from the Suez Canal in the Sinai. The British 5th Mounted (Cavalry) Brigade was in trouble. They had been attacked by the Turks.

Shanahan had to wake Bill, which was no easy task for he loved his beauty sleep. This time the lieutenant exercised his right to 'bribe' his animal with a handful of sweets and a big drink. The sugar helped wake him. It was going to be a long ride through the night over terrain they had never travelled before. Twenty minutes after the call the squadron was lined up in seventy rows of two, including the eight packhorses and mules and two camels at the rear. Shanahan was out front with Bill prancing a little to start with and still smarting from his rude awakening, but after several weeks he had not attempted to buck his new master/friend once, not even in a frisky, unthreatening moment. He was the horse to have at the head of the column. He was the biggest animal in this outfit by a hand (4 inches or 10–16 centimetres), and easily the heaviest and most powerful. Shanahan, at 180 centimetres, seemed to grow much taller in the saddle, and everyone in his regiment recognised him as the best horseman among them. Most had accepted this even before he'd 'tamed' Bill the Bastard, but after he'd taken on and made that exceptional mount an addition to the Anzac force, everyone acknowledged Shanahan's superiority as a horseman.

The two camels laden with stores and weaponry each carried a little more than the horses. Shanahan had tossed up whether or not to bring them. He expected them to be slower than the horses, but it remained to be seen if they could keep within reasonable distance of the column. He planned a nine-hour ride, with ten-minute breaks for both man and animal every hour. A full moon augmented the light from untold numbers of brilliant stars as they began the steady negotiation of the waves of sand. Talking was forbidden. Voices travelled far in the desert night. The only noise was the light, jangling sound of water bottles hitting metal buckles or belts. One cigarette an hour was allowed but only in the first two hours. A pretty sprinkling of a hundred lights moving at ground level could give away the unit's size and direction. Smoking would be allowed in the breaks but only under cover of coats or blankets.

After forty minutes, Shanahan called a halt. The cameleers were told to return with their animals to base. The camels had lagged behind, groaning when whipped to make them move more quickly. Their stores were spread over eight packhorses and mules. It settled in Shanahan's mind that the Walers were superior in all forms of desert warfare, whether moving to a potential encounter or in the actual battle itself. Troopers had reported that the camel's capacity to go long distances without water was more myth than reality. They may well have had the 'tanks' to hold more water and last longer without a drink, but Walers were consistently going further without complaint—they were much quicker. The troopers would use them in any proposed charge, whereas they would never use camels this way. The men also found them far more accommodating animals. Cameleers were known to build a rapport with their animals, but none ever reported the strong relationships that most troopers had with their horses.

'They [the horses] also smelt a hell of a lot better,' Shanahan wrote to a relative, 'their breaths had a certain familiar fragrance. But the camels were best avoided, at either end.'

The endless hillocks, interspersed with the odd mountain, were heavy, slow going. There was no actual track, except for paths through scrubby sections and the occasional oasis inhabited by Bedouins, where the ground was flatter and firmer underfoot. At other less urgent times they might have rounded up these Arabs to stop them warning the Turks of their advance, but there was no time to spare.

Along with the light, this ride seemed blessed with no wind, but as they moved deeper into the desert, they ran into mist. The troopers all wore their coats to fend off the freezing night air which at dawn would give way quickly to burning sun. Shanahan lifted the pace a fraction in the second hour. Bill was pounding steadily up a minor gradient when he stopped dead about eight paces from the top of a rise. He was agitated, whinnying and pawing the ground. Shanahan nudged Bill with his heels but the horse refused to budge. He reared up. He was not going on. Shanahan called a halt to the column as it bunched untidily behind him. At first he wondered if Bill was playing a stubborn game. He dismounted with Mulherin and walked to the top of the rise. Both men peered over the edge and received a shock.

'Christ!' Mulherin gasped.

Below them, visible in the moonlight, was a sheer drop into a ravine. Mist did not allow them to make out how deep it was. Looking across at other massive dunes which were just visible in a grey shroud here and there, Shanahan estimated the drop to be at least eighty metres.

He remounted Bill, patted his neck with more affection than normal and slipped him a sweet, whispering in his ear that it was a 'real thank you *and* a reward'.

Shanahan leant across to Mulherin. 'We never ride again without a black tracker to scout ahead for drops like that,' he said. 'Jackie Mullagh has to join the squadron proper, not just be a trainer.'

Given the pace at which they were travelling, Bill had just saved the lives of at least a dozen men and horses. This was the first time anyone in the squadron had experienced such a prescient action from one of the mounts. They had all heard stories about horses refusing to go on when the troopers were 'blind' to dangers ahead in the desert. Now they believed them. Troopers half-asleep were now wide awake.

Shanahan motioned for the column to turn around.

'I'm very, very pleased you went to so much trouble to acquire your bastard mate,' Mulherin said to Shanahan, who just smiled ruefully. Both men were shaken by the experience. They found a route down the side of the ravine and then resumed travelling in their original direction.

After a five-hour gallop through the desert, the regiment came across several wounded members of the British Cavalry Brigade in the half-light of dawn. They were on foot and had escaped in the night after a battle. The cavalrymen spoke of a one-sided encounter. The Turks had left some 300 British prisoners with a band of Bedouin 'guards'. Shanahan and his squadron, rifles at the ready, galloped on to Oghratina to the worst sight any of the troopers—even veterans of the Boer War and other conflicts—had ever seen. More than 250 British cavalrymen, in various states of dismemberment, were strewn about the town. The camp had been looted, their horses stolen. The Arabs had fled by camel hours earlier and would have melted into the yellow landscape. There was no point in pursuing phantoms in the desert.

Shanahan and his men scrutinised the identity tags on some of the yeomanry.

'Hey, Lieutenant,' Mulherin called, 'have a look at this one. He's a captain.'

Shanahan held a handkerchief over his face to avoid the stench of rotting human and animal remains. Half a day's exposure to the elements and some birds of prey had worsened an already appalling mess. The officer opened the cavalryman's shirt to reveal his bloodstained torso. His shoulder was strapped.

'I think this is the bloke that Bill bucked off on the Gallipoli despatch run,' Mulherin said.

'Captain Bickworth,' Shanahan murmured, 'I think you're right.'

Shanahan and his troopers were sickened and sobered. He ordered a burial detail for the cavalrymen. A short religious ceremony was held.

It was clear to Shanahan and his men that the Arabs, who were being billed by the High Command as 'friends' of the British forces, were never again to be trusted. Some tribes in Arabia may have been in negotiations with the British to fight the Turks on the Hejaz railway, but the

Bedouins wandering Palestine and the Sinai were under Turkish control and in their pay. This horrific, inhumane incident drove home the reality of the horrors of war. The troopers had been through the hell of Gallipoli where some of their squadrons had been decimated. So far in the desert they had experienced the odd firefight and skirmish. Some had been killed. A few had been murdered by Bedouins creeping into their camps at night and slitting throats. All that was frightening enough, but the experience at Oghratina placed the war in a new perspective. The concept of dismembering bodies was totally foreign to them. Until now the level of brutality administered by the Arabs to at least 250 men—the rest having escaped—had been unthinkable. From this terrible moment, the Anzacs believed they had two major enemies in the region.

14

PRECURSOR TO A 'HOT' WAR

An Australian Flying Corps biplane was the first to spot a Turkish army moving west in the Sinai at the village of Bayud, some sixty kilometres from the Suez Canal. It was travelling at a snail's pace towards the important British-held town of Romani. There were 3000 soldiers and 2000 camels in this Turkish 'caravan'. In any coming battle, it was going to be a contest between the effectiveness of the horses against that of the camels. The Turks and the Arabs used both in combat and favoured camels. The Anzacs, except for the Camel Division, believed in their Walers as their secret weapon. They had been turned out so fit and well trained by Paterson's depot that they had coped with the conditions far beyond any expectations, even from the most optimistic horsemen. This development owed almost everything to the way the men treated their mounts. Many had learned to look after them in Australia. In the deserts of Egypt, this care was even more vital.

The encroaching Turkish force was carrying big guns —5.9 inch howitzers—which impeded their progress across the dunes. From the air, the force seemed hardly to be moving. It was retarded also by the heat and the need to stop and find water in the scarce wells at oases and villages scattered twenty to thirty kilometres inland from the Mediterranean coast. The biplane that had spotted this enemy march flew on around the region and picked up two more big contingents. One had about 1000 infantry and a further 2000 camels. The other had the biggest infantry number yet seen: some 3500 soldiers, accompanied by 1000 more camels. They were all heading in the same direction: towards Romani. The sporadic or 'phoney' war in the Sinai had lasted half a year to 19 July 1916, the day of the reconnaissance by that single biplane. The Turks' aim was to take Romani, the most important town east of the Suez. Once the Turks had it, they would move quickly on Cairo and claim Egypt.

The pilot of the spotting biplane flew low over the Australian Light Horse and dropped a message. All regimental officers were informed of the advance. In the coming days intelligence sources in Cairo picked up that the invading army of Turks included 25,000 infantry and 20,000 camels. In desert terms, this was a considerable force. Taking any more men in the challenging conditions would be unwieldy and unmanageable. Food supply would be a major problem although the Turks could always forage for nutritious dates and other fruits. The major obstacle for so many men was water. The enemy army was split into eight contingents to make the water maintenance just manageable, provided that scouting engineers found old wells that could be refurbished and made to run again.

Shanahan was keen to know the make-up of the Turkish force. He had enemy prisoners interrogated. They confirmed that the incoming army was mainly from the Gallipoli battle, including mostly Anatolians, among the best fighters of the Turkish Empire. Learning this, Shanahan wanted to know if Mustafa Kemal would be their commander. He had been largely responsible for the Turks' spirit and drive in defiance of the Allied attack on Gallipoli. The prisoners claimed they did not know.

Shanahan gathered his troopers and informed them of the invading enemy's complexion. This electrified the Light Horsemen. They had been waiting impatiently for this moment. Any thoughts of deserting evaporated. The Anzacs would be desperate for victory. Meeting the Turks in the Sinai would be 'round two'.

'The gentlemen's war is over,' Shanahan told them. 'This will be the real thing.'

The intensity of encounters and small battles increased as the Turks inched closer to their main target until they were twelve kilometres from the line of posts manned by the British infantry in front of Romani. This defence ran ten kilometres south from the sea and faced the lower hills and Romani sand dunes. Shanahan's regiment moved out on patrol east towards the Turks at Oghratina, which, after the massacre of the yeomanry, had been taken by the enemy. He rode out on patrols every day to seek Turkish locations.

One night he was leading a dozen troopers trotting out over the dunes beyond the defence perimeter when Bill stopped. He would not budge. He snorted nervously and this put Shanahan on edge. They were 100 metres from a hill. In silence, he motioned for his squad to dismount. Two troopers took control of the mounts while Shanahan led the rest on foot, crouching low with rifles and pistols at the ready. He indicated the hill, directing half his men around to the left and the others with him to the right. They were fifty metres from their target when about 100 Turks bobbed up in ambush. Shanahan ordered his men to retreat to the horses. He fired at the enemy, covering his men. Turkish fire from several directions hit the sand around them and created sparks. They had been surrounded.

The troopers reached the horses and mounted, only to see more Turks close by. One lunged at Bill's bridle while a second grabbed at Shanahan. Bill reared high, throwing off the two men. In the same action he kicked one attacker in the face. The man groaned and slumped unconscious. Bill began to back off, dragging the other Turk who had gripped his bridle. Shanahan swung his rifle butt, smashing the attacker in the head. The Turk fell and lay motionless. Shanahan galloped off as enemy fire followed him and his men. It was heavy but ill directed. No trooper or horse was hit. They galloped about 300 metres before Shanahan called a halt. He had the horses taken from out of the line of fire and ordered his men to shoot at the advancing Turks, who were on foot. After a twenty-minute encounter, he directed his men to mount up and retreat another 250 metres. The Turks arrived once more and fighting ensued for a third time. Shanahan and his men dashed for their mounts again and backed off a further 200 metres. Without explanation, he next headed north towards the sea for another 300 metres instead of west towards his regiment's outposts. He stopped and asked for someone to make a fire and boil tea.

'What's happening, Major?' a bewildered trooper asked. 'They'll spot the fire for sure.'

'That's the idea, trooper,' he replied as the others gathered around. 'Did you notice how they all fired at us, but not one of us or our neddies was hit?'

'So? They're bad shots.'

'Not that bad. Back there when we first met them, a couple of them tried to pull me off Bill. Would have got me too if he hadn't been strong enough to shake 'em off. But Johnny Turk could have killed me, easily.' He looked up at the expectant faces. 'He didn't, as you can see. They were trying to capture me. They want information.' He paused and added, 'I'm glad they didn't nab me or any of you. Believe me, their methods of questioning would have been far worse than being shot.'

The billy boiled. Two of the troopers poured tea and filled mugs for the others.

'They have been following us,' Shanahan added. 'They want to find out where our defence perimeter is, one way or the other. We'll lead them on a merry dance away from our outpost.'

After five minutes he asked them to mount up.

'We're taking a wide route to near the coast where we'll lose them, and then head back to the outpost,' he said, and jumped on Bill. He stroked his neck, fumbled sweets into his mouth and said into the horse's ear: 'Thanks again, cobber. That's two I owe you.'

'Three, Lieutenant,' the trooper next to him said. 'If he hadn't stopped when he did, we woulda ridden right into that ambush.'

In the last week of July Shanahan and his men braced themselves for the waves of Turks coming at them. He and his regiment were part of the first line of the defence of Romani. Chauvel had 1500 Light Horsemen to hold the line against the 25,000 Turkish infantry. It was going to be a huge battle against the odds. The British commanders insisted on attempting to manage the fast-approaching war from Cairo and Kantara, forty kilometres away on the Suez Canal, which Chauvel worried was going to put him at a big disadvantage as the senior commander in the field. If he wanted reinforcements, which was likely given he was outnumbered so badly, could he get them to arrive in time? If he had to wait for a command from Kantara, a battle might be lost before a decision was made, especially if the commander-in-chief (General H A Lawrence) had no 'feel' for what was happening on the battlefield. Time was running out and the enemy was expected to launch a massive coordinated attack by early August. Chauvel had no choice but to accept the disjointed and unharmonious command from a distance. But there was one advantage to this ineffective direction from above. Chauvel would be left very much to his own initiative.

To that end on 2 August he took a handful of his Light Horse officers, including Shanahan, on horseback to the end of the line of Romani outposts. Shanahan had not seen much of Chauvel since Gallipoli and he noticed the change in the commander's appearance. The experience at Gallipoli and a serious bout of pleurisy there had taken their toll and etched themselves into Chauvel's features. His hair was thinner, his face was haggard and he now seemed every bit of his fifty-one years. The stress of the current challenge was not going to help him. Chauvel had to make a decision on the defence and consider options concerning withdrawal, which was more likely than not given the numbers arraigned against them. He asked his officers for their thoughts.

The 1st Brigade's forceful, restless Lieutenant-Colonel Meredith spoke up. 'We have to take them head-on,' he said. 'Our blokes want the hand-to-hand stuff. They have wanted it ever since Gallipoli.'

'There will be huge casualty numbers,' another officer cautioned.

'There will be anyway,' Meredith replied.

Others put forth their opinions. Shanahan was the only one in the group of seven who said nothing. Chauvel first asked him about his horse.

'Congratulations are in order,' he said, 'taming that mighty beast is a real feat. I saw him on the Gallipoli despatch run. But I'd like to get a close-up look at him. Why haven't you got him with you?'

'He's resting. He's going to be working overtime.'

'How did you break him?'

'With respect, General, I couldn't.'

'Then how did you make him so, shall we say, "compliant"?'

'I earned his respect and friendship.'

Chauvel nodded and then congratulated him further on his promotion to the rank of major. Then he asked for his opinion on tactics.

Shanahan didn't rush to respond. After several seconds he replied: 'There has to be a compromise between defence and strategic backing away.'

There was silence. No one else had stated the 'retreat' option.

'Good God, man,' Meredith blurted after several suspenseful seconds, 'that's so damned negative! If you have that mindset we have no hope of victory!'

'I speak as someone who will be in the thick of the fighting, Lieutenant-Colonel,' Shanahan said firmly, locking eyes with Meredith. 'We have to draw them to us and use our mounts here and there to fall back. The longer we keep them fighting, the better our chances.'

Meredith went to interject but Chauvel stopped him: 'Continue, Major.'

'Their supplies will be limited. They will no doubt attack at night. If we keep them fighting through the night, we will have the advantage in the morning. We have the wells at Romani and in the area. Johnny Turk will be out of water and, we can hope, low on ammunition by dawn. It will be 100 degrees at 6 am.' He paused and added, 'Then they will suffer. Our opportunities for a "win" will occur then.'

Silence followed as the others digested his words.

'I tend to agree with the major,' Chauvel commented. 'I have asked for other brigades. General Lawrence has not been forthcoming with them. I can't even rely on the British garrison troops. They will only help us if Lawrence tells them to.'

Chauvel led the group on a canter about the area for half an hour, then they trotted up to a high sand ridge. They used binoculars to survey the area. The moonlight was good. They could see the most important locations clearly enough. He ordered the 1st Light Horse Brigade, including Shanahan's regiment, to create a 'hockey stick' formation. The figurative top of the 'handle' touched the coast to the north. The curve at the bottom made up the Light Horse outposts which ran west towards the Suez Canal.

Intelligence coming in to Chauvel indicated the Turks planned to surround the entire British force, close on it, strangle it and take Romani, but no one knew whether they would try to break through the Light Horse barrier or make a sweep south below the 'hockey stick', which would mean traversing the Sinai's heavy, steep dunes. Perhaps they would try to do both. They had the numbers but were probably unsure of how many of the Light Horse they would be up against. If they had known it was a relatively small number, they may well have opted to break the barrier as soon as possible, but in the night, an opposition's size would be difficult to judge.

Anticipating they would attempt to crash through the Light Horse, Chauvel set up fixed battery positions. Telephone lines were laid between outposts, which covered five kilometres. He consulted the others on when they believed the Turks would attack. The consensus was either late on 3 August or very early on 4 August. The educated guess from most was that the Turks would attempt to march up the sand gullies of Wellington Ridge, a key point close to the all-important Romani camp. Assuming they achieved that at some point in the night, they would wait until dawn to charge down and destroy the camp. They would then be behind the outposts of the British infantry. Their second objective would be to attack and destroy them, which would put the enemy in control of the British-built railway from the Suez Canal at Kantara. But there was a vital catch: time. They had to achieve all this by mid-morning and gain access to the Romani wells, otherwise the contest could swing back towards the Light Horse.

15

HIGH FIVE FOR BILL— HERO OF ROMANI

'Allah, Allah, Allah!' The Turks screamed a battle-cry as they advanced: 'Finish Australia!'

It was 1 am on 4 August 1916 and the battle for Romani—indeed, the most important step in the battle for Egypt—had begun. The yelling was followed by heavy fire right along the Australian line. At his posts Shanahan ordered return fire. Despite the brave cries, the Turks were not in sight. Everyone was as yet firing blind under a cloud-covered moon, its light diminishing in the earliest hours. At 2 am the sheer weight of enemy numbers allowed them to infiltrate the Light Horse barrier. The Australian squadrons made a decision to pull back. One covered the other as the staggered, slow retreat began. Shanahan, leading a squadron on Bill, was the last to move. He galloped along the line about 400 metres, up and back, firing at the enemy as they appeared, while retreating with the rest of the Light Horse. It was chaotic but, within the turmoil, the troopers were staying with their controlled withdrawal metres at a time.

At his makeshift tent headquarters just three kilo-metres from the action Chauvel was receiving worrying reports. The battle seemed to be going the Turks' way too quickly. He was tempted to bring in the reserve and Light Horse Brigade, which was waiting outside Romani for the order to join the fray. Chauvel sent urgent orders that every commander in the field had to hold his position. No matter how astute the commander, it was the sort of order delivered more for morale than for any acute appre-ciation of the real situation. No matter what was directed now, the sheer superiority of the Turkish numbers was beginning to tell.

After 2 am the battle was Gallipoli all over again, except it was a shifting encounter. The two opposing forces were just thirty-five metres apart, warring in the dark. Shanahan continued to work Bill hard up and down the line, firing and protecting his men as they eased back. The Australians were under strict orders to avoid hand-to-hand fighting, much to the chagrin of many of the troopers. But that sort of engagement would have been fatal for them. Shanahan was galloping close to make sure none of his men broke ranks and charged forward. The darkness afforded him a thin blanket of security, although at times he could not tell his men from the enemy. At about 2.20 am two Turks rushed him, trying to pull him off Bill, who skipped away. Shanahan turned Bill and fired from a few metres, killing one soldier and wounding the other.

'Major!' a trooper called as he galloped up. 'Our west flank has been penetrated heavily. We need reinforcements.'

Shanahan turned Bill around and made a dash west, calling troopers to accompany him.

Shanahan arrived at the westernmost Light Horse outposts to find them swarming with Turks. There were no troopers in sight. He galloped into the post areas with two others of his mounted force only to find Tasmanian Light Horsemen strewn about, all of them apparently lifeless. Despite the gunfire close by, Shanahan and the two troopers with him dismounted to make a quick check of the twenty or so men. They were all dead. Shanahan ordered that his two-man force remount and search the area briefly for survivors before they too could be captured.

The west flank outposts were being pulverised as hundreds of Turks filtered into the area now and Shanahan was about to order the others to fall back when he heard Australian voices. He turned Bill in their direction and called: 'Tassie troopers!'

They responded, but so did the Turks, who cut off Shanahan's gallop in their direction. He was forced to manoeuvre behind a small dune and reload his revolver, with his two companions close at heel.

'Sounds like a few survivors,' one said breathlessly. 'What to do, Major?'

'I'm going back into it,' he said. 'You follow but at twenty yards, and cover me with fire. I'll see if I can find those men and get them out.'

'They won't have their mounts, Major. How—?'

'Just do as ordered and let me worry about rescuing them.'

Shanahan took off again at a full gallop with the two following troopers firing either side of him. He called for the Tasmanians again and had a fifty-metre gallop before they responded. Four men hustled out from behind a dune, their revolvers at the ready. They were all on foot. Shanahan yelled for the troopers to come to him. 'Here, all of you!' he commanded just as several Turks rushed them.

Shanahan urged Bill to go hard. The great horse responded with one of his charges straight at two of the enemy who were trying to surround the troopers. They did not see him coming. One was hit with such force that he was carried forward five metres. He collapsed like a rag doll, either dead or unconscious. The other Turk felt hooves crash into his rib-cage. He dropped his rifle, fell to his knees and clutched his chest. The breath had been knocked out of him, his ribs crushed. Dying or not, his war was over.

Shanahan looked around for his two support troopers. They had been caught by Turks coming from different directions. He yelled for them to retreat and they did so, wending their way back to the main body of Light Horsemen, who were gradually pulling back.

'C'mon, you blokes!' Shanahan yelled to the beleaguered

Tasmanians. 'Mount him!' He slipped his boots from the stirrups. 'Take a stirrup each! C'mon!' Two of the troopers slipped a boot into a stirrup either side. The other two, with Shanahan's help, clambered onto Bill. The horse now took the weight of five men—about 380 kilograms. He had only ever allowed one man on him for any length of time, now the huge Waler had another four 'foreign' bodies that individually he would jettison. Bill was steady during this furious multiple mounting, his only sign of impatience being a loud grunt each time he drew breath.

Shanahan leant forward. 'Okay, Bill . . . move!' he said firmly, close to the horse's ear.

Turks ran from every direction but were kept at bay by the four troopers, who fired their revolvers at the encroaching shadows in the now thin, occasional moonlight. Shanahan urged the horse on. Bill dug his hooves into the sand and began to canter, which was just about the limit of his pace at first. The two men straddling Bill's massive hindquarters hung on and managed to aim revolvers at the Turks following on foot. Their aim was not steady, but their firing had the desired effect of making their pursuers cautious. They soon fell back, unable to keep pace as Bill reached a rise and bounded down the other side. He ploughed on, digging hard and groaning with every stride in the soft sand.

'Go, Bill! Go, cobber!' Shanahan encouraged him as they reached a less undulating run of two kilometres. They heard the pounding hooves of a horseman following, then another.

'Are they ours?' Shanahan asked anxiously.

'Dunno!' one of the troopers called as they squinted into the blackness. Artillery fire lit up the sky and four horsemen could be seen in hot pursuit.

'Might be Turks!' one of the troopers said.

'We can't outrun them, boys,' Shanahan said, 'so let them get closer and then shoot. Aim well!'

It was a tall order given that the four troopers were hanging on gamely to courageous Bill, who was frothing at the mouth so hard that the wind was spraying it back towards them as he pounded on.

'Which troop are you with?' one of the Light Horsemen on Bill's rump challenged as a pursuing horse was within twenty metres. The answer came swiftly when a bullet hit the sand and sent phosphorous light searing across in front of them.

'Get him!' Shanahan ordered.

The trooper fired and missed but the pursuer dropped back when two more bullets whizzed by him from the others on Bill. He stopped, turned and disappeared into the gloom. Soon all four Turkish attackers, who had commandeered Australian mounts after massacring the Tasmanian troopers, dropped back. Bill had a clear run now as he built to a fast clip on the last kilometre into the Australian headquarters at the village of Et Maler, a kilometre in front of Romani. A hundred metres out, Shanahan slowed Bill to a stop and let the four troopers dismount. Each one patted or hugged Bill. He wasn't used to such enthusiastic human affection but was too fatigued to object. Each trooper thanked and praised Bill, aware that the mighty steed had saved them when all seemed lost.

'You both deserve bloody VCs for this,' one of the troopers said, overcome with emotion. He soon joined his mates as they scurried off to see if they could find another four mounts in order to return to the battle.

A littler further on Shanahan dismounted and walked Bill to a water trough near the animal sick bay. He patted his neck and stroked his mane, saying: 'You are a marvel, my mate, an absolute bloody marvel!'

Vets were working on injured mounts at the sick bay. Some horses hobbled, others had wounds from bullets, knives and bayonets. One limping horse was highly distressed. A vet examined a fetlock, took out a revolver and shot the animal in the temple.

Shanahan looked at his watch. It was after 2.45 am. The noise of battle was at its peak and his men were temporarily leaderless. He waited while Bill drank from the trough. He was not normally a big drinker, but this time he lingered, pausing now and then before taking in more.

'You're like a damned camel tonight, Bill,' he said, 'but with good reason.'

With that, Bill proceeded to urinate, forcing Shanahan to jump clear. When the horse was done, Shanahan mounted him and waited for a reaction. Bill seemed unperturbed. He had already recovered.

'Jesus, mate,' Shanahan mumbled, patting and stroking his head, 'you're not a horse of war, you are a horse of iron.'

He felt certain that Bill would object if he was not ready to go again, but instead of protesting, he pawed the ground in a manner that Shanahan knew well. It meant he wanted to move, trot, gallop and even charge. When horses were being retired, injured or fatigued, out of the battle every few minutes, Bill was wanting to get back into the thick of it, if his master so directed. Shanahan began at a trot, built gently to a canter, then settled into a steady gallop as they headed into the battle zone once more.

*

The Turks had assembled a flanking force of some 8000 infantry. They charged the almost perpendicular slopes of Mt Meredith, which overlooked Et Maler, Romani and the sea. It was now pitch dark. The fire from atop Mt Meredith indicated that a small number of troopers were shooting Turks who were clambering up, sending bodies tumbling down the wall of sand. But a flanking attack saw a thousand Turks climbing to the crest. The defending troopers backed away and abandoned their position. It was 3 am. Mt Meredith was under enemy control.

Shanahan's squadron was exposed on both flanks. He arrived to take charge again. Too many of his men were dead or wounded. His instinct was to pull back, but he had to hold the line and wait for another squadron to withdraw to them. By 3.15 am casualties were heavy as Shanahan's squadron was assailed on three sides. He was forced to concede ground. By 3.30 am his men had been pushed back to the waiting horses. The Turks, with bayonets fixed, kept coming and closing in on the Australians and the horses. A few troopers were taken prisoner.

Shanahan kept his receding squadron steady in the chaos. His troopers were mounted and picking up wounded men where they could. They pulled further away from the enemy's staggered but steady advance. It was important for the Light Horse to reform, pull together and give the Turks pause. Shanahan galloped along his jagged line calling the order: 'Sections about—Action Front!' This caused his troopers to turn and close in together. Their reaction heartened Shanahan and the other commanders. At the most critical moment so far in the middle of what was literally the darkest hour, the troopers had shown unparalleled discipline in battle. This lifted the confidence of the outnumbered force. At intermittent points, troopers dismounted and scooped out holes in the sand to create makeshift trenches. They took up positions, lined up their rifles and waited for the enemy encroachment. Word swept the lines of mounted troopers and those who had entrenched: reinforcements would be there soon.

Dawn was just two hours away. Every minute was now vital. Enemy pressure mounted. Turks on Mt Meredith swept the Australian lines below with machine-gun fire. Shanahan galloped about firing at Turks and inspiring his men. Other officers doing similar work had collapsed many mounts and were taking fresh horses, up to eight times in the night. The overweight South African Brigadier-General 'Galloping Jack' Royston, who commanded the

1st Brigade, was destined to go through eleven mounts in the night. But Bill, who would do more work than all those horses collectively, was still running hard when required. At the make-or-break moment in the battle, in which holding the line was paramount, 'the Bastard' was coming through with a supreme, unmatched performance, without complaint. Shanahan kept checking him, realising that even his monumental strength was being tested in conditions no man or horse could really prepare for.

Minutes ticked by. Everyone wondered when Chauvel would commit his reserve 2nd Light Horse Brigade to battle and relieve the 1st Brigade, which had already gone far beyond the call of duty and levels of fatigue acceptable to any human or animal in any encounter. But Chauvel was not going to be pushed, nor would he be panicked into a decision. He preferred to hit the Turks with his reserve force at dawn. He believed his one big chance to win would occur when the sun grew menacing and Turkish water bottles emptied.

At 5 am the battle had been raging for three hours. The Turks believed it was theirs to be won. After taking Mt Meredith their main attention had shifted west, where the strong Turkish left flank was driving between Mt Royston and Et Maler. It was heading for the railway behind the main British base at Romani. At the same time the enemy on the east had outflanked the entire 1st Brigade, including Shanahan and his shrinking squadron. He was down to about half his force, with the balance killed, wounded or captured.

16

SHANAHAN TAKES A BULLET

At dawn, Chauvel waited until sunlight bathed the entire battleground before he mounted at the head of the 500-strong 2nd Light Horse. Royston, on his eleventh horse, was behind him. In full view of the beleaguered 1st Brigade and the Turks, the long column wound its way from Et Maler. The troopers in the field and on the defending plateaus and ridges cheered.

Chauvel did not order a gallop. He was content with a steady canter through the sand, keeping the horses fresh and the troopers ready, if impatient, for battle. Yet the unhurried non-charge had its own menace for the Turks. They had slogged through the night only to be met at first light with a demoralising sight. They themselves were in need of relief and water. Neither was forthcoming; there was only the promise of a brutal sun, diminishing food rations, reduced ammunition and ferocious opposition. The Turks had the numbers and much of the high ground but now the prospect of victory was no certainty. Chauvel's tactic had changed the battle dynamic. His column advanced steadily towards Wellington Ridge directly in front of Et Maler, the last bastion before Romani.

Chauvel rode up to Lieutenant-Colonel Meredith on the ridge just as a Turkish infantry contingent reached a ridge in front of them. He wasted little time in ordering Royston to send two regiments (384 troopers in each) to shore up defences to the west. The first hour of dawn would now decide if the Turks could be held.

Shanahan was at the bottom of Wellington Ridge with his and other regiments trying to stop the enemy onslaught above them. The Turks opened up with artillery. He saw a fellow officer shot dead a few metres from him. Shanahan fired at his assassin but was caught in an ambush close to the foot of the ridge. He was shot in the thigh, but kept fighting for another hour, protecting and covering his troopers as they withdrew. Then he slumped unconscious on Bill. When the horse realised his rider was not directing him, he took off at a canter, building to a light gallop, through the lines, heading for Et Maler. Had he bolted at full stride, he may well have caused Shanahan to slide off.

Bill galloped the two kilometres to Et Maler and stopped outside the vet hospital area at about 6.15 am. There was so much activity with injured animals that Bill was not noticed for several minutes. Shanahan was found unconscious, his left leg soaked in blood. A vet led Bill to the soldiers' hospital tents. Shanahan was laid out next to a long line of wounded men waiting to be seen by a medico. His leg was dressed and he was placed on the critical list along with scores of other men from a battle that was still intense.

Bill was taken to the horse yard and placed with the reserve horses. He was given a long drink at a trough and fed. Sergeant Sutherland was in charge of this modest remount depot of about 3000 horses, the reserve for the 1500 troopers. He knew of Bill's effort earlier in the day in carrying out the five troopers. He was soon informed that Shanahan was wounded.

'Put "the Bastard" wi' the packhorses,' he ordered an assistant. 'He is not to be given to anyone for more action. That wee neddie has done enough. He's earned a break. If Major Shanahan can't ride him again, Bill's combat days are over. He'll become some lucky officer's best packhorse.'

'What happens if Galloping Jack wants him?' the assistant asked. 'He's been barging in here every half-hour wanting a replacement.'

'You don't let him have Bill.'

'But the general is so bloody demanding that—'

'You tell him from me that Harry Chauvel has given the order: no one touches Bill the Bastard.'

'Jesus! Has he?'

'That's beside the point, laddie. Anyway, I don't think General Royston would be stupid enough to attempt to saddle up Bill. He wouldn't want to look a fool if he was thrown off in front of his men. "The Bastard" will never let anyone mount him for any length of time except the major.'

*

At 8 am the Turks had taken Wellington Ridge but the British artillery gunners had found their range and were pulverising the position. The enemy was forced to abandon it. After six hours of gruelling battle, the Turks had been halted. With the sun pounding down and no chance of them proceeding, Chauvel called for rein- forcements. As he feared, the British infantry, sitting in outposts, would not help the Light Horse unless General Lawrence ordered them to do so. But communication lines to him were down. Chauvel now had an anxious wait for help from the New Zealand Mounted Infantry (Light Horse), British cavalry, another Australian Light Horse brigade and English cameleers. With the slow communi- cations, these forces would not arrive until early afternoon. That left Chauvel galloping up and down the lines with Royston, exhorting his men to make extra efforts to hold out right along an extended front running ten kilometres almost to the coast.

*

By early afternoon Shanahan had regained conscious- ness but his condition had deteriorated. Overworked doctors pronounced him 'dangerously ill'. They discussed amputating his leg but thought he was too weak for an operation. Medicos had to make quick decisions for hundreds of casualties. The plan for Shanahan was simple: if he recovered they would again consider amputation.

*

The reinforcements arrived between 2 and 3 pm and were immediately deployed to fight off the Turks, who by late afternoon were struggling everywhere. The enemy had anticipated taking the wells near Romani, but that was now impossible. They were out of water and food almost all along the front. The Turks would have to withdraw, defeated. Chauvel revelled in the thought that Romani was the first decisive victory attained by British land forces in the war except for campaigns in West Africa. The Light Horse primarily had denied the Turks in this critical battle, which meant Egypt had been saved for the British. He praised his senior commanders, but it was the disciplined men such as Shanahan and horses such as Bill that had done the courageous hard work in combat against all odds. They were the difference at Romani.

Thirteen days later, at dawn on 17 August 1916, three Australian doctors examined Shanahan, who was sitting up in bed in a hospital tent at Et Maler. He asked about Bill.

'Bill?' the thin-faced medico in charge asked. 'One of your men?'

'My mount.'

'Oh, Bill the Bastard!' the doctor said, his pale grey eyes twinkling and expression lightening. 'He is a damned legend! You collapsed while fighting at the bottom of

Wellington Ridge. That amazing beast brought you back, but not to us—to the vet!'

Shanahan managed a wan smile. 'He is okay though?'

'Far as I know, fit as a fiddle. Sergeant Sutherland is recommending him for some sort of award. A horse VC!'

'My men . . .? My troopers?'

The doctor began opening a large hold-all. He placed a saw on a table below Shanahan's eye level. Other cutting instruments were put beside it.

'Don't worry about them for the moment. You'll be briefed on everything.'

'The battle . . .?'

'We won, although you wouldn't know it from the carnage of man and beast that was out there. But it was all over the day you were brought in by Bill.'

'But where is he?'

'No idea. He may be in Katia by now. The whole force has cleared out. They're chasing the Turks back to Palestine. But don't worry about that mighty stallion. Sergeant Sutherland is telling everyone that General Chauvel has ordered that he never fight again. He has earned a long life. He's a packhorse from now on.'

Shanahan was not yet mentally strong enough to comprehend this. It was confusing. Why was his steed being made a packhorse again?

'You're going to be okay,' the doctor reassured him, 'but I must say you had us worried. Thought we'd lose you a couple of nights ago. But you're a very fit man, Major.'

'But my leg has to go?'

The doctor took a deep breath. "Fraid so. We couldn't operate until now. But it's gangrenous.'

'Yeah, I realise that. It's green and putrid.'

The doctor nodded. A nurse closed the tent flap. The whiff of ammonia dominated the operating theatre.

'Take heart, Major,' he said, 'you lived. And you're not alone in losing a limb. I've come from the Western Front. I reckon 100,000 Allied soldiers lost one limb, at least, in this year alone.' He sighed. 'I know. I removed my share of them. But that's good for you. I do know what I am doing.'

The comment was not comforting. Nurses came into the room with other medical equipment.

'I know it's not much consolation, but remember maybe a further five, perhaps six million have died in action since 1914. Surviving is something in this war, Major.'

'Life is a fair consolation,' Shanahan said. 'I'll take it.'

The doctor didn't respond. His mind was off small talk and onto his speciality with a saw.

'Let's do it,' Shanahan said, a twinge of regret in his stoic voice.

A solemn-looking, plump nurse stepped forward holding a morphine syringe. 'Lie back please, Major,' she said, with more of a wince than a smile.

17

STUMPED BUT
NOT OUT

A few weeks after the amputation, Shanahan was taken
to an Anzac hospital at Abbassia, two kilometres from
central Cairo. He had come to terms with his fate, but it
did not console him that he was out of the war. He longed
for his mates, the camaraderie and combat. Now all that
had been taken from him. But he was philosophical. He
was forty-six, not sixteen as some of the Light Horsemen
were. Shanahan had lived a full life. Losing a leg was not
the devastating event that it would have been for someone
younger and in his prime. He had come through Gallipoli
and now the Sinai: eighteen months of war experience,
much of it in frontline action. He had lived long enough
to comprehend what 'luck' was. He had been lucky to
make it. The doctor who removed his leg had been right.

He couldn't now be killed in combat. Ten million others would not be so fortunate.

He would have felt much better if the war was over. He wouldn't miss anything if it were. Yet the Turks had only just been beaten and pushed out of the Sinai. There was still expected to be at least one more year of battles before the realisation of the aim of the Anzac Light Horse: to push the Turks right back over their own border. This meant defeating them in Palestine, Arabia and Syria. It was a tall order. Shanahan's frustration was in knowing that he would not be part of it.

He, like every trooper, had heard the rumours filtering down from the Australian command, led by Chauvel. If he got his way, the objective would be achieved. Revenge against the Turks would be complete. The main obstacle preventing this from happening was the British High Command in Cairo. General Murray, a fine peace-time commander, did not have the will to defeat the Turks on a grand scale in war. His lukewarm approach meant the enemy would always be allowed to regroup after defeats such as at Romani and would remain a threat. The Australian approach, in crude terms, was to chase them and wipe them right out, then the problem would be dealt with and the war in the Middle East would be over. But Murray would not go anywhere near that solution. He preferred to supply generals on the Western Front with men and equipment when asked. This always kept his own British force in the Middle East restricted. It was also frustrating for Chauvel and Co. 'It [the British High Command approach] was like being half-pregnant,' Shanahan wrote to one of his brothers in Australia, 'and one can't really be in that condition.'

He had plenty of time for writing as he stayed in the fifty- by thirty-metre hospital with its high wooden crossbeams, white walls and rows of beds along two walls. Shanahan was told he would never ride again: his left leg had been removed halfway up the thigh, which would make getting on and off a horse very tough. Shanahan did not agree. He said nothing but worked hard at his physical condition, getting used to exercising minus a limb. He could do press-ups and sit-ups, and there were dumbbells in the makeshift gymnasium at the back of the hospital. Shanahan would rise at 4.30 am to work out for the last hour before dawn when it was still cool. He prac-tised jumping from a tree stump, the sort of movement he anticipated when dismounting. He built extraordi-nary strength in his right leg. His only problem was the nerve endings in the stump. Night and day there was pain in a foot, a calf, a knee and half a thigh that did not now exist. It could be excruciating, causing him to wake sweating in the night, swearing that the leg must have grown back. He would throw off his sheet to see that it had not. But none of the nurses in the Abbassia hospital ever heard him complain. He would call for large doses of aspirin, shake his head in bewilderment about his 'ghost of a leg', as he called it, and say nothing more. The nurses who looked after him—Sisters Wallace, Brown, Reid and O'Neill—knew he was suffering. They saw the sweat on his sheets and pillow. They heard him cry out in the night while asleep but never when he was awake. They admired his courage and attitude. His strong character quickly caused him to be their favourite patient. One—Sister O'Neill—was rumoured to have a crush on him.

Shanahan was buoyed by a steady stream of visitors. His Light Horse companions had little to do beyond patrolling after pushing the Turks out of the Sinai. There would be no attack on the Turkish stronghold of Palestine's Gaza on the coast until at least the early spring of 1917, so it was back to the 'phoney war' of a year earlier. His close mates such as Mulherin and Legg visited every other day. They were allowed to take him into Cairo a few times after he had been in Abbassia for five weeks. He used crutches, his one strong leg serving him well as he hopped along with his mates at the bazaar and haggled with stall owners over food and other items.

His spirits lifted when he was told that Cath Phelan would visit him in a few days. Shanahan spent the time carving out a miniature wooden doll's house. It was about thirty centimetres high and included tiny dolls. He had Sister O'Neill create small white and black dresses and tiny red and black hats for them, which replicated her appearance on the two occasions they had met.

'Who is this present for again?' the big-busted, large-hipped Sister O'Neill asked when it was completed.

'A friend from my early life in Queensland,' Shanahan replied, as usual giving little away. The gift was wrapped in paper and covered by a silk shawl he had bought in a Cairo market.

'A girlfriend?' the sister asked, trying to sound casual.

'No, no. She's engaged to a bloke.'

Phelan arrived at the Abbassia hospital looking her spectacular self in a loose floral dress, yellow hat and white shoes. She swept up to the front veranda, bringing with her a waft of perfume and a big bunch of flowers. She joined Shanahan and they sat on wicker chairs under an awning that provided shade from the mid-morning heat.

Phelan handed the flowers to Sister O'Neill, who said frostily: 'No longer than half an hour, now, please. He's having too many visitors . . .'

When she disappeared into the hospital, Shanahan rolled his eyes and said: 'You can stayer longer if you want. I'm fine.' He scrutinised her. 'You're looking so well.'

She patted her stomach. 'Eating too much.'

'Booze puts it on too, you know.'

'I know.'

Before she could say how fit he looked, he handed her the gift. She unwrapped the shawl.

'It's lovely. I do like the colours!'

'That's part of it.'

Phelan removed the paper on the doll's house and examined his handiwork.

'Oh, it's beautiful!' she said. 'Where did you get it? The market?'

'I made it.'

'Oh,' she mouthed, speechless. She reached across and hugged him, kissing him on the lips. Shanahan responded.

'Thank you. Thank you so much.' Her eyes welled up. 'No one . . . no one has given me such a beautiful thing.'

Shanahan was touched but kept his composure. 'Don't know about that,' he said. 'I'd put the Rolls marginally ahead of this. But thanks for liking it.'

'Like it? I love it!' She hugged him again.

Stony-faced Sister O'Neill bustled back and served them tea and biscuits. She tapped her watch.

'Not too long,' she said with a cold stare at Phelan, 'not too much excitement.'

She strode off, her large posterior wobbling with intent. Phelan stifled a giggle.

'She's wrong,' he said, 'I want lots of excitement. Lots of distraction.'

'That reminds me,' she said, putting down her tea. 'Won't be a moment.'

Phelan hurried to her car and returned with a carton of books.

'You told me you were a big reader.'

'Great!' he said, examining some covers. 'I am devouring one a day in here.'

They chatted about some of the volumes. She admired the doll's house again.

'Do you carve things for a hobby?'

'I play around with it when I have time. And it's in surplus right now.'

'Have you done other things here?'

'A few.'

'Can I see them?'

'Aw, they're not too good.'

'Please?'

Shanahan sipped his tea.

'Sister!' he called.

O'Neill joined them.

'Could you bring me my . . . er . . . carving, please?'

'What? The three of them?'

'No, the last one; the biggest one.'

O'Neill returned with a wooden horse, which stood at about the height of the doll's house.

'I know who this is,' Phelan said, turning it around. 'It's Bill the Bastard, and it's good! I think you shaped the dimensions about right. The big shanks, the long neck.' She held the sculpture close. 'That's his face alright.'

Shanahan looked embarrassed.

'You miss him, don't you?' she said, putting the replica Bill on a chair.

He sipped his tea. 'There is no one on him,' he said, nodding at the sculpture. 'That's the way it is.'

Phelan took out a small hip flask and tipped some whisky into her cup. Shanahan noticed but said nothing.

'Like father, like daughter,' she said with a grin. They chatted for another fifteen minutes before Shanahan took out a rusted silver fob watch and glanced at it.

'Should I go?' Phelan asked.

'No, no. Just checking. The sister is strict.'

As he was speaking, Sister O'Neill's heavy tread shook the veranda once more.

'We'd love more tea, please,' Shanahan said, jumping in first. 'Miss Phelan is staying another half-hour.'

The sister glared at both of them but dutifully removed the tray with a noisy rattle of cups and plates and left.

Phelan pointed to his fob watch. 'I recall you were awarded that for something,' she said with a frown.

'Your memory is a little scary,' he said.

'May I see the watch?'

'Why?'

'It may have an inscription.'

'It was a long time ago, Cath.'

'May I see it?'

Shanahan detached it from his shirt and handed it to her. She turned it over. There was an inscription on the back, scratched and faded.

'What does it say?' she asked.

He shrugged.

Phelan took out her glasses and held the watch close.

'"To Michael Shanahan . . ."' she began, squinting, '"for courageous . . ." can't read that word . . . oh, "service . . . to Roma during the floods of . . ."' She put down the watch and removed her glasses.

'I remember now,' she said, smiling slowly, 'you built a boat at the height of the floods. No one had need of boats where we were. You used it to ferry people to safety— hundreds of them!'

'Noah's minor ark,' he said.

'Was it big? I recall it as smallish . . .'

'Just bigger than your average dinghy, but it did the job.'

The tiny and less obtrusive Sister Wallace arrived with fresh tea, having replaced O'Neill. When she had stepped daintily away, Phelan smiled mischievously.

'There was another thing we didn't discuss when we spoke last,' she said. 'I didn't forget, I was nervous about bringing it up.'

He waited.

'Just at the time of the Depression in '93, there was a cattle rustling gang roaming the bush around Roma. The leader was a young buck who wore a handkerchief over his face so he would not be recognised. He and his gang used to steal cattle from the big properties in the region and give them to the poorer folk. He became known as a sort of Robin Hood of the Queensland bush. We heard that this gang was operating until about '96 or '97, long after we left Roma for Brisbane.'

She paused to scrutinise his face. There was not a flicker in it, not even an eyelid blink. He remained his expressionless self, even more granite-like than usual. She looked away, putting her hand up to shield her eyes from the sun to see if she could spot the pyramids, which shimmered like a mirage in the desert.

After a moment, she went on: 'This Robin Hood had a nickname.' She turned to face him again. 'He was known as "The Bloke".'

'What?'

'The Bloke.'

'Wait a minute, this bloke—this Robin Hood fella—was known as "The Bloke"?' Shanahan pulled a face. 'Not much imagination there. He must have been a pretty ordinary sort of cove to get such a flat, dull sobriquet.'

'A sobri what?'

'Sobriquet. Sort of like a nickname but stronger. An epithet.'

'Epi . . . stop there, please! Nickname is enough.' She bit into a biscuit. 'You read too much. I shouldn't bring you so many books.'

'I'm just an uneducated bush lad,' he said, 'left Roma State School at fourteen.'

'I'm an overeducated vet who is semi-literate. Too many equine science reports, not enough literature reading.'

Phelan studied him. 'One other thing I recall from those early Roma days,' she said with a frown, 'you ran for mayor in '93, didn't you?'

'No. I was *asked* to run for mayor. Never ran. Politics was not for me. Besides, I was too raw, too young.'

'You were twenty-three, right?'

'About, yeah.'

'Why do you think there was such a push for you, then?'

'Don't know.'

Sister Wallace reappeared. She stood close to Shanahan and tapped her watch.

'Just a few minutes more, Sister,' Shanahan said.

When Sister Wallace had departed, Phelan held his hand. 'I want to take you to see Bill,' she said. 'He's back at Moascar. I spoke to Banjo yesterday. The Light Horse won't need him until April.'

'Might not need him at all. I'm told the British infantry will dominate the attack on Gaza.'

'Will you come to Moascar?'

'The medicos are pretty strict. They say I can go to the Cairo markets, and that's it.'

'Then I'll take you to the market, say, tomorrow at 11 am?' Phelan smiled devilishly. 'Who knows where my lovely car will take us after that?'

18

GETTING BACK ON THE HORSE

'I need a chair,' Shanahan said to Paterson.

'Sure, we can all sit outside the tent,' he said, smiling at Phelan.

'Not to sit on,' Shanahan said. 'I want to stand on it.'

Paterson looked confused.

'I am going to mount him.'

'No, Major, I can't allow that.'

Phelan touched Paterson's arm. 'Please let him, Banjo.'

Paterson blinked and smiled resignedly. 'Let's see how the Bastard reacts,' he said, trying to maintain his authority while keeping Phelan happy. 'He has been more bad tempered than ever since your separation. We couldn't feed him a couple of times and he went on a sort of water strike for a few days. He kicked Sergeant Sutherland, which he never did before.'

'Aye, it was more than a friendly tap,' Sutherland confirmed with a rueful look.

A trainer began to lead Bill out of the corral area. He reared up and refused to go through a gate. Three other assistants hustled to assist. He was unruly and uncooperative as the four trainers approached with him. They held on to him. He whinnied in protest, then went quiet. His nostrils twitched.

Shanahan, aided by two sticks he had fashioned himself, moved a few paces towards him. The horse took a few hesitant steps his way. Then he trotted to him, head down. It wasn't in supplication or a charge. Perhaps it was curiosity as his instinct and memory clicked together. He stopped a pace from Shanahan. Bill's head stayed down, allowing Shanahan to stroke his neck.

'You okay, cobber?' Shanahan said. 'You look in good nick.'

Bill pushed his head towards Shanahan's trouser pocket, looking for sweets. He was a little too boisterous. Shanahan lost his balance and fell over. Phelan and Paterson moved to pick him up but he wouldn't let them. Instead Shanahan used his right leg and sticks to stand. He climbed onto the chair and stood balancing on the seat. He motioned for the four trainers to bring Bill close.

'Wouldn't it be best to ease him round a bit?' Paterson asked.

'Got to do it now,' Shanahan said. He slipped his right boot into the stirrup and mounted Bill. The trainers backed away. Bill was frisky. He pranced a few metres. Shanahan fought the reins, trying to keep his balance in the saddle by leaning his body in the direction of his amputated leg. He felt as if his left foot was struggling to slip into the stirrup. He glanced down twice. At this moment more than any other, he felt as if the foot was still there, but it was more memory than tingling pain. He had been on a horse almost every day since he was a child, apart from the past six weeks. He was six when he first managed to ease his feet into short stirrups while riding a pony. Forty years on, the sensation of those 14,000 riding days would not leave him. Perhaps they never would. That phantom foot missed the stirrup too.

Shanahan kept chatting softly to Bill, leaning his head close to the horse's left ear. Bill jerked his way round the yard, forcing the others to jump clear. Shanahan used all his skills to keep control without responding to the horse's testing of him. Bill broke into a canter. Shanahan attempted to pull him back a fraction. Bill reared up, though not really in anger or irritation. Shanahan's centre of gravity was all over the place without the left leg. He slid down the saddle onto the horse's rump and then slowly off, landing on his right leg. He fought to stay upright with a couple of hops along the ground before falling. Bill stepped away, apparently not sure if he should bolt or stay.

Shanahan asked a trainer to bring his chair and sticks to him. He stood on the chair again. The four trainers manoeuvred Bill over to him as though they were trying to put him in an imaginary stall at a race meeting. The horse resisted a little, almost as if he was enjoying this new mounting 'game'. Shanahan got astride of him a second time. Bill did not move. Shanahan's right stirrup heel caressed Bill as it had every day, three times a day, for their short but intense four-month partnership. In that time they'd had more than 300 rides. They had been constant companions through hot days and freezing nights. Now Bill trotted around the corral in complete contrast to his behaviour minutes earlier.

Shanahan wanted to take him into the desert. Phelan demanded that she ride also. Paterson had Bill's partner, the gentle mare Penny, saddled while Shanahan put Bill through some paces. It was all coming back to both of them.

'Reminds me of the Portuguese bullfighters mounted in the ring,' Paterson observed. 'I'm told by Sergeant Mulherin that's how they fought together—total control, man and beast in symbiosis. No matter who came at them and with what, they darted about as one.' He sighed regretfully. 'It took a bullet to finish it.'

'That wee neddie is totally wi'out fear,' Sutherland said. 'Just like his pal on him.'

'I can feel a ballad coming on,' Paterson said.

'Really, Banjo?' Sutherland asked hopefully.

'They are poetry worthy,' Paterson said with a tilt of his head, 'but sadly the muse left me about twenty years ago.'

'Maybe this sort of moment brings it back, hey, Banjo?'

'It should, Sergeant, it should. But verse other than dogged doggerel is an emotive thing. To me, it's the purest form of writing.'

'Perhaps one day when you reflect on it, it'll come.'

Paterson grunted a laugh. Sutherland knew from long experience that it signalled a cynical comment.

'Trouble is,' Paterson said, 'not much you can rhyme with "Bastard". At a stretch—mustard, custard, rusted, busted and dusted. Oh, and lusted. We mustn't forget lust, ever.'

They watched as Phelan and Shanahan cantered out of the depot, heading for an oasis about two kilometres east.

'I envy the bastard,' Paterson mumbled.

'Yeah, me too.'

'I don't mean Bill,' Paterson said, turning to enter his tent office.

*

'Like it here?' Phelan asked as she held her cocktail up to Shanahan in salute.

They sat at a wicker table under an awning on the veranda at the front of the ancient, four-level Shepheard Hotel in Cairo. It was 9 pm. Shanahan had been away from the hospital for ten hours.

'Heard about it,' he said, swirling his spiced tomato juice, 'lots of history.'

'I love it!' she said. 'You can watch the passing parade of Egyptians. You can see the VIP guest coming up the stairs. I could sit here sipping these concoctions all night.'

'I believe you,' Shanahan said.

'Bob introduced me to Winston Churchill here last week.'

'Winston who?'

'Don't be funny.'

'After Gallipoli he's no mate of any Australian's,' Shanahan remarked.

'He paid the price: lost his job over it.'

'I lost plenty of cobbers over it. They paid a bigger price.'

'He was with a funny little Englishman dressed in Arab clothes. Somebody Lawrence. Bob says he is a spy in the Arab Bureau, trying to whip the Arabs into action against their Turkish masters. This fellow says an uprising may end Turkish control in the region.'

'You can tell Bob from me to tell his little mate Winston that only a force like our Light Horse will smash the Turks and drive them out of Palestine and Syria,' Shanahan said. 'You have to hit them head-on and beat them. The Arabs don't fight that way. They do it by "hit and hide" methods. That won't work. The Turks have had them bluffed and under their control, more or less, for several centuries.'

Phelan seemed to sense a certain vehemence in him. Was he bitter and frustrated over not being part of the Light Horse push? She was about to change the subject when a dapper little general stepped lightly up the hotel steps.

'Is that . . .?' she began.

'Yes, General Chauvel.'

He spotted Shanahan. Instead of entering the hotel, Chauvel walked to him as he struggled to stand.

'No, Major,' Chauvel said, 'don't stand.'

Shanahan introduced Phelan.

'I won't interrupt,' Chauvel said, 'just want to tell you that you will receive the Distinguished Service Order, for your performance on 4 August at Romani.' He shook Shanahan's hand. 'Congratulations. Very well deserved. It will be gazetted early in the New Year.'

Shanahan saluted his commander-in-chief. Chauvel nodded to Phelan, turned on his heel and entered the hotel.

Phelan kissed Shanahan and congratulated him. 'DSO, a big honour!' she said. 'It's just short of a VC, isn't it? He clearly appreciates you.'

'It's mutual. If the British commanders were half as good we'd finish this war inside a year.'

'I wanted to tell you something,' she said. She sipped her cocktail, building courage. 'I'm getting married.'

Shanahan looked surprised but hid any disappointment. If he had been ambivalent about taking the relationship with her further, he wasn't now. He was attracted to her beauty, vivacity and probably her compassion where he was concerned. But he would have had worries about aspects of her behaviour, especially her excessive drinking.

He raised his glass: 'My turn to congratulate you!'

'Thank you.'

'Who is the lucky bloke? Banjo?'

'Huh!'

'You never did tell me about your date with him.'

'Nothing to tell.' She paused. 'He likes a drink.' She smiled approvingly. 'He did recite a ballad when he'd had a fair bit of champagne.'

'Called?'

'"The Bastard from the Bush".' She lit a mini-cigar and spent a moment fitting it into the holder. 'He has an *unusual* mind, hasn't he?'

'That ballad was by Henry Lawson, not Banjo.'

'Okay, so I'm not up on my Aussie limericks,' Phelan said. 'He still has a risqué mind to repeat it to me.'

'Bush literature is full of it. You just never read it in *The Bulletin*.'

Phelan sniggered. 'One verse did tickle me,' she said. 'I can recall a couple of lines . . . "The stranger made this answer to the captain of the Push, Why fuck me dead, I'm Foreskin Fred, the bastard from the bush." That's all I can remember.'

Shanahan's expression brightened. He finished the verse: "I've been to every two-up school from Darwin to the 'Loo, I've ridden colts and black gins, what more can a bastard do?"'

She sat back and sucked gently on her cigar. They watched the street. A man with a monkey was making the animal do smoking tricks with cigarettes. A hotel flunky moved them on.

'I thought you were on the permanent engagement list,' Shanahan said.

'I was, but . . .' She patted her stomach.

'Oh, I see. How far gone?'

'Didn't you notice I was bigger?'

'No . . . I just thought it was a bit of healthy condition.'

'Well my "condition" is five months pregnant.' She looked away, pretending to watch people walking up the steps.

'Do you know whose it is?'

'It's Bob's,' she said indignantly, making lingering eye contact.

He sipped his drink. 'We last "met" in April,' he said slowly. 'That's five months.'

'I know. But it's not yours.'

'You certain?'

'Yes.'

'Hmm,' he murmured as he stared at her. 'Well, they say a woman knows.'

'Bob has work in Paris. I'm going with him.'

'When?'

'Next week.'

'That's when they're sending me to hospital in London. They call it "recovery".'

'Will you keep in touch?'

'Sure.'

Phelan reached across and kissed him warmly. 'I'd like that,' she said.

Phelan glanced at her watch. 'Bugger!' she said. 'We better get you back. Your nurse girlfriend will be annoyed with me.' She drained her glass. 'Just one other thing. You were "The Bloke", weren't you?'

Shanahan chortled but remained enigmatic.

'Why won't you say?' Phelan said. 'It's twenty years ago!'

Shanahan reached for his sticks. 'Nothing to tell,' he said, hoisting himself up.

'It's why you were so popular. Why the poorer end of town wanted you to be Roma's mayor.'

Shanahan smiled. 'I think you are going to tell it the way you want to,' he said, 'whatever I say.'

Later, when Phelan was driving away from Abbassia, she happened to look at the back seat where her dolls, the doll's house and the shawl were sitting. Placed in the middle of them was the wooden replica of Bill with an envelope tucked under its feet. Phelan stopped the car by the side of the road, opened the envelope and read the note from Shanahan:

Thought you might want little Bill. I really appreciate what you did in getting me and big Bill together. But we don't have much use for each other anymore, so I thought you might like him, as a thank you.

A kiss for the other one that got away . . .

Michael.

Phelan rested her head on the steering wheel and cried.

19

THE MOODY BULL

'I hear you have a rather special stallion at the depot,' General Sir Edmund Allenby said to Paterson. The *great, lonely figure of a man*, as Paterson described him, relaxed a little in front of this old acquaintance. The ruddy-faced, moustachioed, 193-centimetre Allenby had been fired from the Western Front and been given the Eastern Front—Egypt and Palestine—as a consolation, replacing the ineffectual General Murray. The balding, 56-year-old Allenby had been storming about Cairo since his recent arrival, putting fear into every officer and soldier. Even at Moascar he had bawled out trainers and cooks and anyone else who displeased him.

'Stallion?' Paterson said, feigning ignorance.

'Some monstrous Waler that no one can mount,' Allenby said, tapping his boot with a riding whip. 'A real hero at Romani, I'm told.'

'Bad luck, General. He's out on manoeuvres.'

'Oh is he, Paterson? Pity. Let me know the second he returns. Want to get a good look at him. May even ride him meself.' He pulled at the brim of his cap, which was jammed on his forehead, adding to his formidable appearance. 'Or at least get a cavalryman to have a go.'

'Of course, General.'

They walked away clear of Allenby's cowering staff of ten and chatted about the Boer War, where they had first met.

'How are you, General?'

Allenby glanced over his shoulder, making sure none of his people could hear him.

"Fraid I'm becoming very hard to get on with. I want to get this war over with.' He slapped his boot with the whip and jerked his head to indicate his staff. 'If anything goes wrong I lose my temper and cut loose on them.'

They wandered to the horse corral.

'Don't go for your Walers much,' he said, squinting around the paddock. 'They're a common, hairy lot compared to the horses your lancers brought to South Africa.'

'To be fair, General,' Paterson said, 'those horses were a select group of police mounts in superb condition.'

'Have you brought any over?'

'A few. But we couldn't get enough of them to make a difference in this war.'

'But this motley lot,' Allenby said, waving his hand at a field containing hundreds of Walers, 'they're not going to win a bloody war either!'

'They were a big factor in belting the Turks six times in the Sinai.' Paterson began to number them on his fingers. 'Romani, Katia.'

'Oh, yes, yes,' Allenby said, cutting him off impatiently, 'but what about Gaza 1 and 2? They didn't do so well there!'

Paterson didn't know if the general was baiting him or not. 'Are you serious, General?'

'Of course I'm serious, man!' he said, his complexion flaring up. 'I don't joke about war!'

'As I understand it, General,' Paterson said carefully, 'the Light Horse and cavalry were sidelined for those battles. It was more an infantry encounter.'

Allenby's nose twitched. He was not used to being corrected or contradicted. Everyone, even prime ministers and other generals, tiptoed around him. Paterson was allowed some slack. He was an old friend. Allenby respected him as a poet, and Allenby loved poetry.

'They were in it,' he said archly, 'they should take the blame too.'

'With respect, General, you are replacing a commander-in-chief who was not up to it. That's where the real problem with Gaza lies. Not the infantry and certainly not the troopers and my Walers. The infantry had it won. Murray and Lawrence, sitting in Cairo, panicked. They believed the Turks were sending reinforcements. They were not. The

Light Horse was about to ride into Gaza for the coup de grâce when they, and the infantry, were pulled out. It was a classic case of snatching defeat from the jaws of victory.'

Allenby drew himself up to his full height, towering over Paterson. 'That's what you think, is it?' he asked.

'Everyone in the army knows this,' Paterson said quietly, surprised that he had not already received a rebuke. Instead, Allenby swivelled on his feet and tapped his boot with his whip once more. His face was still dangerously red, as if he might explode. Paterson braced himself.

'I like the way you say "my Walers", Paterson,' Allenby said, calming himself, 'but I wouldn't be so proud of 'em. Good God, I've seen better nags pulling milk-carts in London! They have poor breeding and it shows. Cross-breeds all! Draughthorses and Timor ponies in there too! Terrible! Thoroughbreds perform better. Breeding is everything!'

'With respect, General, we are not trying to win the Derby here. We want stayers in really trying conditions. Horses with guts. Breeding is one thing, character is another.'

Allenby looked back towards his staff. He had given Paterson enough of his precious time.

'You may not have had time to study the record in the Sinai,' Paterson persisted bravely. 'When you do, you will see three things. First, the Light Horse were magnificent against massive odds in battle. Second, you have the best general on the front in your command.'

Allenby arced up. 'Who, General Chauvel?'

Paterson nodded.

'I may well be relieving him of his command.'

'Why?'

'None of your business!'

'He may not meet you at eye level, General,' Paterson said, 'but he has what you need to win this war.'

Allenby glared in a way that suggested an impertinent Paterson had stepped over the line. He turned on his heel and began to march off.

'I haven't told you the third thing!' Paterson said, raising his voice as Allenby strode back to his staff. 'You won't win without those bloody milk-cart pullers!'

Allenby kept walking and was soon in front of his staff.

'I want to see the infantry's 10th Division!' he bellowed as if he was addressing others beyond the group. Paterson wandered over. He was about ten paces behind Allenby. He pulled out a small notepad and began to scribble, thinking this moment might make an article. It would be censored now but not after the war when he could publish it to show a little of the character of the commander-in-chief.

None of Allenby's entourage could tell him where his 10th Division was. He received blinks, blank looks, diffident coughs and a couple of his staff began studying their feet.

A brave young officer piped up that it was on its way from India. No one was certain if it had arrived in a camp near Moascar. Allenby, known without affection as 'Bloody Bull', snorted.

An even more courageous staff man stepped forward. 'If you please, sir.'

Allenby cut him off. 'I don't want to hear you talk!' he snapped.

Paterson shook his head slightly as he took down every word.

Allenby stepped up to the officer, looking as if he might strike him. 'I have enough men following me around to staff the whole British army and you can't find me a division!'

Paterson was distracted by Sutherland.

'I'm told you were looking for Bill,' he said quietly. 'He is back from the exercise he was on.'

Paterson raised a finger to his lips. 'No he is not,' he whispered, glancing at Sutherland. 'I don't want this bullyboy going near him. Keep Bill out of the stable. Put him up the back of the paddock with the mules.'

Half an hour later, Allenby entered Paterson's tent office. His face colour was still up. He was agitated. Paterson stood up from his desk and saluted.

'You have some impressive horseflesh hidden in the stable, Paterson,' he said, tapping his boot with his whip even more often than before. 'They've got a bit of breeding in 'em. Where did you get 'em?'

'I bought them, General.'

'You mean you purchased them with remount funds?'

'Out of my own funds.'

'Oh, royalties for "Waltzing Matilda" have come in, have they?'

Paterson remembered telling Allenby in South Africa that he had earned a pittance from his songs and poems.

'They are my property, General.'

Allenby leant forward, his knuckles on the desk. His manner was menacing. 'You bought them from wages earned in the employ of the British army. You have maintained them with funds from this British army depot. They belong to the British army!'

Paterson was incensed. He was about to tell him he would take them home after the war, but checked himself. Allenby was looking to exact retribution from *anyone* for his 'deployment' away from centre stage of the Western Front. Better not to rile him, Paterson thought.

'I have receipts for them, General.'

'You know what you can do with them! Those horses are British property. They will stay with the army even after this bloody war is over!' He flicked his whip at flies. They irritated him, as did the sand and heat. They added to his fury at being effectively exiled to the desert.

Paterson held his tongue. Allenby stormed out and began raging yet again to his cringing staff about his 'lost' 10th Division.

20

CHAUVEL'S SECOND MASTERSTROKE

General Allenby was a more cautious commander than his aggressive demeanour implied. He took half a year to make a third attack on Gaza. Impatient as he was, he knew that a third failure to break through the Turks at this stronghold on the coast would mean he would have no hope of achieving his aim of driving the enemy from Palestine. His own record would be as a losing commander after his 'demotion' from the Western Front. But the careers of others hinged on this battle too. Chauvel had the best record by far of any of the generals in the field. His 6–0 battle score against the Turks in the Sinai had the respect of everyone, including, eventually, Allenby himself. Despite his gratuitous remark about Chauvel being fired, Allenby knew on reflection that he had to rely on the Australian.

At first Chauvel's quiet defiance of Allenby's demands raised his ire, but Chauvel refused to let Allenby link directly to Australian Prime Minister Billy Hughes to demand men, money and equipment. Chauvel remained loyal to British General Birdwood, who was the connection to Australian prime ministers and had been since Gallipoli. He was one of the few British generals the Anzacs respected. Allenby was furious that he would have to go through Birdwood for any demands. He was hostile to any of the Western Front High Command generals who had conspired to dump him and send him off to the sideshow in the Middle Eastern desert. He hated having to treat them diplomatically to gain what he wanted. But once he stopped fuming over Chauvel standing his ground, he looked more objectively at what lay ahead.

He had a chance to win at the third battle of Gaza for two reasons and they were both commanders. One was Chauvel, whom Allenby now chose to run the Desert Mounted Column: 34,000 horsemen made up of 70 per cent Anzac troopers and the rest mainly British cavalry. They would attempt to smash two Turkish armies and sweep across Palestine. The other 'reason' for his chance to win Gaza was British espionage operative Major T E Lawrence, who told Allenby that if he was given enough guns and gold, he could induce the Arabs in Transjordan and Arabia to keep a third Turkish army occupied on its Hejaz railway. It would be distracted so much, Lawrence convinced Allenby, that it would not be able to support its brother armies in Palestine.

This had transformed the depressed, vituperative, grumpy Allenby into a man of more than hope that he could achieve something historic with the help of these two different but brilliant commanders. But first he had to win Gaza. After the now-sacked British generals had sidelined the horsemen at the failed battles, he reinstated them. The plan was to make a feint against Gaza with the infantry. Then there would be an attack by Chauvel's Light Horse that, it was hoped, would take the village of Beersheba, seventy kilometres south of Gaza, and allow a quick, concerted assault on Gaza itself.

On the big day, 31 October 1917, Chauvel waited, as he had so effectively at Romani, until the very last moment to send his reserve Light Horse into action. But then he pulled the most spectacular surprise of the war so far. The normal modus operandi for the Light Horse was to charge close to the Turkish trenches, dismount and make their move on foot. It was what the Turks and their German masters expected, so the wily Chauvel ordered a charge *without stopping*. Some 800 horsemen would ride right at the 4400 Turks armed with artillery, machine-guns and rifles. They would attempt to obliterate the opposition in trenches and the village 1.5 kilometres beyond them. Allenby, about twenty kilometres away, was apoplectic over Chauvel's delay. He sent blistering commands to him to *attack*. Chauvel threw the missives away. At 4 pm he gave the order to Brigadier Grant. He was to lead the charge to the trenches.

Young Ben Towers, the first person known to have stayed on Bill for more than two minutes, was a machine-gunner in the Light Horse line-up readying itself for the charge. Seeing his nerves, an older trooper next to him said: 'You'll be okay, son. We gotta take that town. If we don't, we are well and truly stuffed. The wells are there. We must get the horses to 'em. Otherwise we have to back off ten mile or so to other wells. The next hour will tell everything.'

Packhorses and mules were trotted up behind and roped to the troopers' horses. They carried their machine-guns and ammunition. Towers did a double-take at the big pack animal assigned to him.

'Jeez,' he said to the trooper connecting him up, 'that's Bill the Bastard!'

'Yeah, you got the best packhorse in the business. Lieutenant McNee has been wounded.'

'I've ridden him!'

'Yeah, yeah,' the trooper said dismissively, moving on to the next machine-gunner with a mule. 'You'd be the first after Major Shanahan.'

'I was the bloody first!'

The trooper was too busy with his job to respond.

Moments later, the order came down the lines of the 800: 'Regiments! Form squadrons, line extended . . . form squadrons, line extended . . .'

Towers spoke into the ear of his own beloved Waler, telling him he would be getting a drink soon and trying to calm him. But the horse sensed something else. He could smell fear. It put both his rider and him on edge. The squadrons trotted towards the area behind Chauvel's command post on a hill with a 'dress circle view of the show', as he characterised it. The general was there in full view of his select horsemen, who were about to make history or be consigned to oblivion.

The German officers in charge of Beersheba's defence were standing behind the Turkish trenches. They watched the build-up from a sandy knoll. They believed that it was a mere demonstration. The Germans were on the record as saying the Australians were madmen but they were not crazy enough to charge. Besides, they had no real history of the British conventional charge as such. The Germans had done their homework. The troopers who wore the emu plumes in their hats were horsemen who could shoot. They were not British cavalry. They would always dismount and advance on foot. That approach would be accomplished now after dark, which would mean their strike would fail.

From the enemy's point of view, the Light Horse's first squadron emerged in a line 1100 metres long over the top of a hill, then three kilometres south-east from the trenches and less than five kilometres from Beersheba itself. It was 4.30 pm and the light was already fading fast. The horse vanguard came over the crest of the hill.

Orders were barked to the Turkish artillery men. Wheels were spun and the big gun barrels lowered. The gunners gave the order to fire.

Ben Towers was shivering. He was in the front squadron of the biggest body of horsemen in a century to line up for a cavalry-style charge. They began at a slow walk,

five metres apart. A corporal next to Towers gave him a
'thumbs-up'. Everything was going to be fine; the thrill of
a lifetime. Towers glanced back at Bill the Bastard. His
clever-looking head seemed to express that he was relaxed.
Towers felt a strange sensation with this recognition. His
nerves quietened for the moment. He was surrounded by
strength among the troopers who did not look scared.
Behind him was the most powerful animal he had ever
encountered. The horses always gave the troopers confidence. They acted as a kind of shield for what they were
about to run into. None cared to think that in a flash a
bullet from a Turkish sniper, or a round from a machine-
gunner, or a carefully calibrated shrapnel spray, could pull
down his defences.

Seconds later the front line of troopers was thirty metres
short of the crest. The brigadier commanding flexed his
arm, extended it towards Beersheba again and bellowed:
'Forwaaaard!'

The troopers roared like a crowd at a bullfight and
advanced.

By the time Towers reached the top of the hill they
were at the trot and in full view of the enemy. He looked
around. Bill was close, bunching with him. On his left
flank were artillery, other machine-gunners and reserves.
Ambulances were behind them. A reserve Light Horse
regiment brought up the rear.

Any independent observer would have thought the
Australian charge was sure to lead to disaster. The heavy
firepower awaiting them seemed too much to break

through. This opened up when the Light Horse was clanking forward at a canter three kilometres from the trenches. Turkish machine-gunners began spitting out their bullets at a fearful rate accompanied by a 'rat-tat-tat' sound. The troopers heard it, but as nothing hit home initially, they cantered on, impressed by the 'display' lighting the dusk sky. It was hard to believe that it was fire aimed at them. Continuous rifle flashes outlined the position of the enemy trenches. Their field guns now came into play beyond and above the rifles, delivering the bigger, deeper light emissions.

An Essex artillery gunner on the left of the Australians used binoculars to find the source of this early fire coming from a hill almost in a direct line with them. The British officers did quick calculations. They calibrated the range and let the big guns loose. Their shells burst like a row of red stars over the enemy defence lines. By fluke or good management, the first shower of shells killed all the Turkish machine-gunners on the hill in question. It was only the beginning but it was significant. The odds improved marginally for the attackers. A direct impediment had been eliminated before close contact had been made.

Two-and-a-half kilometres from the trenches, the commander who had taken up the forward-most position pushed his arm out straight and yelled: 'Chaaaarge!'

The troopers quickly reached a gallop. Towers could feel his heart thumping. He glanced left and right. Troopers were screaming invective. The rope to Bill the

Bastard had gone slack. Towers looked back for a split second to see that the massive mount with the big weight strapped onto him was pushing close to his Waler's hindquarters. It seemed to want to crash through and take the lead. No other pack animal was so close to his assigned trooper.

Towers heard a cry to his far left. A fellow rider had been hit. There was a thump ahead of him to the right. A horse had been struck. By the time it was down, Towers' mount, and Bill close behind, were past it. Towers looked straight ahead now, not wanting to take in the sight of his fellow troopers and their mounts going down. Over a slight rise he could see Turkish riflemen propped 100 metres in front of the lead horses. Some managed further shots, but they were their last acts as marksmen. The rampaging horses barrelled straight through them. Towers felt his rope to Bill go taut. Bill had veered to avoid a Turk but had collected him with a dull thud, leaving him limp and exposed to trampling by scores of hooves.

The horses' tempo increased. Their nostrils widened. They could smell the water in the precious wells of Beersheba. That is what they cared about. They had no fear, not even of the German planes swooping low above them and rolling out bombs. Pilots were finding targets difficult to set up in the fading light. Whether or not the troopers had been confident or had harboured hidden fears at the start, they were buoyed now. Some of the enemy machine-gunners had been silenced. Turkish riflemen had been trampled on. The troopers waved their bayonets. They were inspired. There was a sense that they were going to overrun the trenches. The waves of troopers were more or less intact.

Red and orange flashes seemed to Towers to be whizzing close. He could smell cordite. It was strong. There was an overwhelming odour of something burning. It was so thick in the air that some of the troopers were gagging and clearing their throats. Suddenly Towers was hit. He fought to stay in the saddle, but fell hard. His horse reared and wanted to go on, but Bill put a brake on him. The two horses stopped about thirty metres from Towers. He put his arms up to shield his head as troopers swooped by. A bullet had hit high on his right femur, shattering it. His twisting fall to the broken soil had mangled his leg. Towers passed out from the pain.

The troopers careered on, building to a racing speed half obscured in clouds of reddish dust. Their pounding hooves could be heard in the trenches as a low continuous rumble, like thunder. Chauvel, watching from his balcony seat on a hill three kilometres away, thought his force 'seemed to move silently, like some splendid, swift machine'.

Either the Turks had failed to change their rifle sights at this point, or they were poor shots. The troopers were not being felled in significant numbers. Some 500 metres out, they could see the shallow front trench, with unfinished earthworks nearby. The Turkish riflemen forward of the trenches saw the rolling ball of dust with the long line of bobbing horses. Their choice was simple. If they stayed in place they risked almost certain death. Most ran to rocks for protection.

The front horses were at a full gallop. They were not stopping. The Turks could hear the harrowing cries from the Australians in the lull of artillery fire and over the machine-guns. The bush cries and cooees would have been unintelligible to the Turks, but the intent was clear.

German and Turkish officers accepted for the first time that they had been duped. The Australians were not acting in a conventional way. They were not going to dismount. They were charging straight at the trenches. Time to make a hurried exit. The Germans began scurrying back towards Beersheba town. Two were assigned to blow up the wells, which would deny the attackers an important goal.

The Light Horse hurdled the first trench. The startled Turks were unable to get in a clear shot at even one mount. The troopers attacked the second, wider, deeper trench, but the men in that were too stunned to fight back. Few took shots and even fewer were foolhardy enough to lunge up at the bellies of the leaping horses. The Turks recovered some composure in and out of the trenches and fired at the troopers. In the ensuing closer combat, some troopers and their horses were shot down.

In the field, ambulance vehicles were bouncing around looking for fallen troopers. They found young Towers, still unconscious, his leg a mess and already the target of a thousand flies that feasted on congealed blood and exposed bone. Placing him on a stretcher, the medicos were shocked by a lone Turkish gunman who had wandered close. He pulled out a revolver and fired at them. One of the Australians pointed to the Red Cross markings on the ambulance. The Turk ignored him and fired at the stretcher. He missed and hit a tyre on the ambulance. It hissed flat. The Turk kept moving and was soon out of sight over a rise.

One medico ran to the horses. Towers' Waler was fretting and sweating. The medico turned to Bill, who stood by placidly. The ambulance driver helped the medico remove the ammunition boxes and machine-gun equipment from him. They stretchered the barely conscious Towers onto Bill and tied him on. The medico mounted Towers' Waler and moved off slowly. Bill made no sign of protest. He seemed to regard the prone trooper on the stretcher as a 'load' rather than someone trying to ride him. He trotted along obediently, head down and untroubled, to the field hospital.

Meanwhile the fighting at the trenches was bloody. The Anzacs were unforgiving, especially after several incidents in which troopers were killed by Turks who had previously surrendered.

One German engineer reached vital installations with demolition charges laid ready at the wells and main buildings. He was chased by a trooper who caught up to him just before he could throw a switch that would have set off most of the charges. The trooper aimed his revolver and shouted options to his quarry: 'Stop or I'll shoot!'

The German hesitated. The trooper stepped forward until he was four metres from the German. He put his hands up. Only two of the seventeen wells were blown, and the bulk of the Walers would be watered that night in Beersheba.

Soon almost all the horsemen broke through and overwhelmed the Turkish trenches, making it the most successful large-scale charge in the last 200 years. The attack claimed thirty-one troopers and seventy-one of their horses. Exhausted troopers, adrenalin still pumping, watered their horses at Turkish troughs and then fell on their knees to drink beside their thirsty mounts.

*

'How did we go?' Ben Towers managed to ask as a doctor administered morphine and then completed dressing his leg wound. Towers was in excruciating pain. A moon-faced padre with a nervous eye tic entered the tent and sat by the young trooper.

'We took the town' the padre said, attempting to sound free and easy. 'You've been part of a terrific victory.'

Towers was doped and delirious. The padre's breezy words did not seem to register.

'Are they at the trenches? Are they fighting?'

'No, that's all over. The blokes and horses are enjoying a good drink.'

Towers screamed in pain. After a moment he asked: 'What about my Waler?'

'They're all okay, Ben, don't worry.'

'Bill?'

Thinking he was referring to a fellow trooper, the padre assured him: 'Bill's fine, really well.'

'Bill the Bastard!' Towers yelled, and attempted to sit up. The startled padre eased him back down on the pillow.

'Yes, the bastard,' the padre said airily, again thinking he was speaking of another trooper.

Towers lapsed in and out of consciousness through the night. He made it to the morning, but only just. The padre returned, his tic now a never-ending blink of nervousness. He would be with the youth at the end.

'My name is not Towers, it's Burke,' he said, 'I'm Ben Burke. Please make sure they get the tombstone right!'

The padre's rapid tic could not hold back his tears. He gripped the young trooper until he went limp. The next day, he was buried in a temporary cemetery on the outskirts of Beersheba.

Soon afterwards Fred Burke of Cootamundra received a telegram from army headquarters informing him of the death of his 'nephew' Ben, who had joined the Light Horse in 1914.

Burke wrote back to the army: 'I do not have a nephew named Ben. I do have a son by that name but I believe he is somewhere in the Northern Territory droving. We have not heard from him for three years. In any case, he couldn't be in the army. He is only 17. That means he would have been 14, just, when he joined up. You have made a mistake.'

21

RESTART

Shanahan wrote regularly to Paterson and his mates Mulherin and Legg and received news from them about the progress of the Light Horse through Palestine as they pushed the Turks back. He always asked for news about Bill and was delighted to learn he had survived Beersheba and was again with a group of packhorses picked out for senior officers.

Shanahan had made his own progress. He completed hospital rehabilitation and gained a job in an office in London's Victoria sorting out allocations of Australian Soldier Settlement Blocks of property for servicemen when they returned home. It was a job not without importance, although it was largely clerical. His debility limited his options and he decided it was futile trying to re-establish himself as a carpenter or builder.

A perky, auburn-haired cockney woman, Charlotte Lampkin, joined the office as a typist/clerk. More vivacious than beautiful, the 26-year-old was of medium height and full-bosomed. Charlotte had the odd experience of being introduced to five men without the full complement of limbs, three who were missing legs and two with amputated arms. They had also been set up in administrative work after being injured in battle and forced out of the Australian army.

The fifth man she met was Shanahan. He was the only male to stand for her when they shook hands.

'No need to get to your feet,' Charlotte said.

'I didn't,' Shanahan said, 'I've only got one.'

Charlotte giggled. 'Cheeky!' she said, creating an immediate rapport. 'And weird,' she said.

'Why?'

'Never met an amputee before,' she whispered.

'Bit disarming?'

She began to agree and then saw the joke. 'You are so naughty, Major!' she said. 'I think I'm going to like you.'

Later on her first morning she walked past Shanahan, smiled, and then looked back to find him ogling her shapely calves.

'I saw that,' she said, 'you're only jealous.'

'What?'

'I've got two,' she said.

Shanahan gave a hint of a smile. Humorous exchanges

had been few and far between for him in the last year. He had become despondent waiting for the war to end so he could take a boat home. He was grateful for every letter but each one put him in a maudlin mood. He hated not being involved with his cobbers and the men in his former command in the desert. Each report indicated the Light Horse was headed for glory sooner or later. They were beating the Turks at every encounter. It was a slow, painstaking business held up by lack of supplies, bad weather and the superior numbers of the enemy. There were grumbles from Mulherin and Legg, but they also conveyed a certain satisfaction in the Light Horse's achievements. They were gaining their revenge after Gallipoli. There had been several charges after Beersheba, which had already (only six months after the event) lodged itself into Australian folklore.

'But our charges are always against fixed positions and trenches,' Mulherin wrote to him, 'and you may be amused to learn that the Turkish cavalry has hardly been seen in fighting against us. We reckon they are scared. We have learned from captured German cables that they believe we are truly madmen, and I quote, "who will go where no man or horse should go". Reckon they might be right too. But we think the Turkish cavalry has taken the German appraisal to heart. They won't come out and play.'

*

A friendship began between Shanahan and Charlotte. They both had flats at Marble Arch, north London.

Shanahan lived alone and Charlotte stayed with her two older sisters.

In conversations during the morning tea break, she peppered her comments with references to a 'Stanley'. Shanahan asked about him and was told that they were 'nearly engaged'. 'He just hasn't popped the question yet,' she told Shanahan, 'but he will.'

'What's his name?' he asked.

'Stanley Butler.'

'I should have guessed.'

'What do you mean?'

'All butlers in England are called "Stanley", aren't they?'

'Oh, you!'

'Don't tell me he's a manservant?'

'No, he's a stockbroker's . . . er . . . clerk.'

'Hmm. Didn't serve?'

'Failed the medical. Lung problems.'

'Does he smoke?'

'Too much.'

Shanahan bought a motorbike with a sidecar and rigged up a pulley system connected to the steering to allow him to drive it with one foot. He asked Charlotte to ride with him to Hove on the south coast one weekend. She said she would like to but that she had to be true to 'Stanley' even though he was 'in Scotland grouse-hunting with friends'.

After knowing each other for two weeks, one mild winter's afternoon they walked from Victoria to Marble Arch, and then decided on a further stroll to Bayswater Road, nearly as far as the farm at Notting Hill Gate. A pretty young girl was walking with a milk pail, selling milk. Charlotte bought a bottle. When they returned to Marble Arch, she asked Shanahan if he would like to come in for tea and meet her 'spinster' sisters, Ruth and Rebecca. Both the corpulent, dour women seemed taken aback at meeting Shanahan. He stayed at the flat for an awkward half-hour during which the sisters grilled him about his intentions. Would he return to Australia after the war? What trade would he take up? Wouldn't he be restricted because of his disability?

'Have you ever been married?' Ruth asked as Shanahan took out his fob watch, looked at it absent-mindedly and seemed not to hear. Ruth was about to repeat the question when he stood up.

'Sorry, ladies, must be going,' he said, and shook hands. Charlotte accompanied him outside.

'I apologise for them, Michael,' she said.

'The tea was okay,' he said brightly, 'and that milk was so lovely and fresh.' He touched her on the shoulder. 'I understand their concerns. They wouldn't want their beautiful little sister disappearing halfway round the world with a one-legged stranger! Their home would be much less attractive.' He kissed her warmly on the cheek, held her close and added, 'Even quite plain, really.'

She looked up. 'Bit previous, aren't we?' she said with a coy look. 'Who said anything about me going halfway round the world?'

'Why not? Australia is a fine country.'

'I've known you just a few weeks!'

'So? It's time to know what you want.'

'What *you* want, perhaps.' Her hand went to her mouth as she tried to repress a smile. 'You are quite wicked, really!'

Charlotte returned to her flat. The three women sat in their living room discussing him. Ruth asked her why she was friends with him.

'The major is a lovely man,' she said, realising that they had not approved of him.

'You're not dumping Stanley?' Rebecca asked.

'No, Michael is just a work friend.'

'That's where he should stay, then,' Ruth remarked tartly.

'What's wrong with him?'

'C'mon, Charlotte! You're not blind!'

'Spill it out then,' Charlotte challenged them, 'why do you object to the major?'

'For one thing,' Ruth said, 'he has to be twenty years older than you.'

'Didn't know there was an age barrier to friendship!' Charlotte snapped back.

'He is also an *Australian*,' Rebecca said.

'He has manners, he is charming . . .'

'He hardly opened his mouth. Talk about a man of few words!'

'He's shy.'

'Weak, if you ask me,' Ruth said.

'Michael is a war hero! He has the DSO.'

'They give them out to staff officers,' Ruth sneered. 'Harry Baker was—'

'Not anymore. Michael got his for bravery in the field.'

'*So* he may have told you,' Rebecca mumbled.

'I've seen the citation!' Charlotte took out a handkerchief. 'You two are really horrible!' she sobbed.

'We just don't want you to give up Stanley Butler,' Rebecca said.

'I think you are both jealous!'

'Let's be frank, Charlotte,' Ruth interjected, 'he is an old Australian cripple with few prospects.'

'We are just friends!'

The sisters glanced at each other.

'Come, Charlotte, we saw the way you were together,' Ruth said. 'Very cosy. Mark my words, that man has designs on you.'

22

BANJO'S REBUKE

'Bloody Bull!' Paterson said, screwing up a letter and throwing it at a bin. 'The bastard!'

Sutherland was in the office going through files.

'What's wrong, Major?'

'Allenby has made it official. No horses will be allowed back to Australia at the end of service.'

'Why?'

'Aw, bullshit about the mares not being able to breed on returning home in case they had disease. What disease? Arrant nonsense! There's other mumbo-jumbo from the "Horse Demobilisation Committee" in the damned London War Office. How would those bloody grey pommie bureaucrats understand anything about the bonds between the troopers and their mounts?'

Sutherland retrieved the screwed-up paper near the bin and read it. 'Jesus!' he exclaimed. 'They want to sell them to the British or Indian army.' He shook his head. 'I wouldn't be letting the lads know this. They'll go on strike.'

'Read the last paragraph. It's fucking "Top Secret!"'

'You know what it means?' Sutherland remarked after scanning the one-page letter. 'The troopers won't give them up. They will shoot them rather than hand them in. Besides, we know that the older neddies will be sold for meat in Cairo.'

Paterson sat at his desk. He frowned, thought for a minute and then asked: 'Do we know where Allenby is now?'

'Camped at Jericho. We had a cable last night. His staff wants a suitable horse—one that is "placid yet big and stately"—they said.'

'What for?'

'He's going to give out medals to the Anzac Mounted Division. Doesn't want to drive up in his Rolls. Wrong image to present to our troopers. He wants to ride up to them.'

'It's a wonder he didn't ask for my Khartoum or one of the other thoroughbreds.'

'I think the "big and stately" suggests that.'

'Who's running the remount at Jericho?' Paterson said, reaching for the phone.

*

The heat was oven-like at the Jordan River in May 1918. There was a lull in the fighting before Chauvel's mighty force would again pick up the pursuit of the Turks after pushing one enemy army north beyond Jaffa in Palestine and another east to the Jordan. Allenby was surprised at the position the Light Horse had put him in after taking Jerusalem. When he was dumped from the Western Front, British Prime Minister Lloyd George had put great store in him 'taking back Palestine, and in particular the Holy City of Jerusalem' from the Turks. George was then a new prime minister looking to do things differently in an attempt to take the British public's mind off the tremendous carnage on the Western Front. He foresaw a psychological boost for the British in securing Jerusalem, never mind that it was a trifling military acquisition when compared to the struggle for even yards on the Somme in France. Christians and Jews were thrilled at the snatching of the Holy City from the Muslim Turks. It was not billed as a holy war but that was the underlying theme in George's emphasis on the sideshow in the Middle East.

After those early months of anger from Allenby, the success against the Turks since Beersheba had the big man less hostile and more amenable. He let Chauvel run the campaign in the field and only issued broad direc-tives to him. He indulged the enigmatic T E Lawrence in his messianic support for the Arab cause. He gave him guns and gold, as requested, to bribe the various tribes into supporting a roughly unified Arab force that ran terror tactics against the Turkish army garrisoned in forts right along the Hejaz railway. The effect, as Lawrence had promised, was to keep that army in the forts and to disavow them the chance to move into Palestine to help the other two armies.

Chauvel and Lawrence kept the faith yet Allenby remained impatient, constantly asking Chauvel to get up to strength with men and horses in readiness for a two-pronged thrust to smash those three Turkish armies. But the commander-in-chief was aware that a previously unlikely success was now more than likely. He took time to hand out decorations for actions in the field. He knew that the Anzacs thrived on victory. They needed incentives and inspiration. With this in mind he had 5000 Australian troopers lined up on their mounts at a parade area near a road five kilometres from Jericho. The same number of infantry in lines together was something to behold, but 5000 horsemen, all wearing their slouch hats with the striking insignia of emu feathers, approaching from three metres above the ground was awe-inspiring.

Chauvel, Allenby and English Brigadier-General Trew were chauffeured to the division's HQ just out of view of the waiting mounted troopers. Allenby was strangely nervous. His staff sensed this, as did Chauvel. He knew he was the figurehead of the British armed forces in the Middle East. He would never be loved or adored by the troopers, yet his size, demeanour and aggressive nature were a contrast to his indecisive predecessors, who were rarely seen at the front. And when they did turn up, they were treated with barely restrained disrespect. Allenby projected a warrior-leader image and it was appreciated by all who wanted to fight and win. For these reasons, he was especially self-conscious on this occasion, the first time he had been in front of such a big number of the troopers, and the first where he would give out medals to them.

'What horse have you got for me, Harry?' he said as he alighted from his Rolls. Chauvel motioned to three troopers who clip-clopped across the road with three riderless, saddled mounts. The one designated for Allenby was the biggest. Allenby examined it.

'Deep, tight girth,' he said, pushing his finger under the leather belt round the horse's body which secured the saddle. 'Long rein. In fact, unusually long rein. Hmm. Haven't seen such an expensive bridle . . . Rolled leather and brass buckles no less! Reminds me of those used at my polo club.' He looked around at the trooper who had brought him the horse. 'Did you saddle him, trooper?'

'No, sa! Remount people did it, sa!'

Allenby ran his hands over the horse's left hind leg.

'Knees and hocks could be lower,' he mumbled, almost to himself. 'Not a bad animal. Huge barrel, good head.' He stood back. 'Damned big! Eighteen hands, I'd say.' He stepped closer to the horse. 'Hmm. Very good head indeed!'

Allenby turned to Chauvel. 'Waler, is it?'

'It came from our remount depot so it must be, Edmund,' Chauvel replied, preoccupied with examining his own mount before lifting himself onto it.

'Never seen one quite as big as this,' Allenby observed as he walked around the horse. 'Got a name, has it?'

Allenby looked to the troopers who had brought them the horses.

'Ah, he's called William, sa!' one of them said.

'William?' Allenby repeated.

'Yes, sa!'

'Not *King* William, just plain William, eh?'

'He is a Waler, sa!'

'Ah yes. You Australians do have a penchant for simplicity.'

Allenby hoisted his big frame into the saddle. The horse did not move a muscle.

'Not much life in 'im,' Allenby mumbled as he adjusted his derriere in the saddle. 'C'mon then, William, you sleepy old thing. Let's get going!'

The horse stood stock still. Allenby was sweating in the heat. He twisted in the saddle and belted the horse on the rump. He swung his stirrups hard into the animal's flanks. It put its head down and its tail stiffly out and charged straight off the road.

A small section in the right-hand corner of the lined-up mounted troopers could see a disturbance near HQ. One witness saw a horse 'head down, tail straight back, pig-root for the bush in a ball of dust'.

Allenby had lost control and was just hanging on. Chauvel took off after him, praying the chief would not be bucked off. In a sudden flash Chauvel recognised the horse by its ferocious charge. It was *Bill the Bastard*. Chauvel had last seen him from a distance on the despatch run at Gallipoli. Bill wheeled in a semicircle back up to the road and down the other side, allowing Chauvel and his speedy mare to cut across close to him. Chauvel reached for Bill's rein and held on. Bill slowed to a disgruntled trot, then a walk. A shaken Allenby took the moment to slip off and step away as Bill kicked back. The Rolls motored to them. Allenby was sweating profusely, his heart racing. Shaken, he slipped into the back seat of the vehicle, trying to regain some composure and dignity. None of his staff was brave enough to say a word.

Meanwhile Brigadier-General Trew's horse had been spooked by the incident. Chauvel let go of Bill's reins and galloped after Trew, who had also lost control. Chauvel soon settled Trew's Waler and trotted them back to HQ. They passed Bill, who was standing quietly by the side of the road chewing on some low scrub as if he was an innocent bystander. Chauvel had a quick consultation with his staff.

'Find a rider who can take that mad horse back to the depot at Jericho!' he said, fuming. 'I don't want to see it again.'

'Only one bloke can ride him, General,' a staffer said. 'He's a blackfella, sir, with the troopers: Jackie Mullagh.'

'Pull him out of the parade, give his horse to the commander-in-chief and tell him to get "William" out of sight, otherwise the horse may be shot!'

After a further twenty-minute delay Allenby—settled on Mullagh's mare—Chauvel and Trew trotted onto the parade ground. A cheer went up from the troopers.

Allenby, happy with his replacement horse, leant across to Chauvel. 'Is that a reception of derision, Harry, or are they just happy to see us?'

'Don't believe it's necessarily insincere, Edmund,' Chauvel said. 'I think they are like us. They don't like being kept waiting half an hour in 100 degree heat.'

'Quite,' Allenby said as the cheering died down.

Chauvel wished to know how Bill the Bastard could have been selected for the most important rider in the entire British army on the Eastern Front. The troopers who delivered the mount said they had just picked up the horses selected by the depot officer in charge. The depot officer said it had been a simple error. A trainer in the Jericho depot had followed instructions from Moascar to find a 'big, stately, placid Waler' for Allenby. The trainer said that the second biggest Waler in the depot was a very quiet pack mare named 'William'. She was a chestnut, like Bill, who some knew by reputation to be something other than placid.

'Why is a mare called "William"?' Chauvel wanted to know.

'She is very big and strong for a mare,' the depot officer replied, 'but you'd have to ask Moascar because she came to us months ago. She was always called William.'

'Who ordered the horse for General Allenby?'

'I didn't take the call, General, the trainer did.'

The officer said Bill was a much-respected 'power' packhorse of remarkable strength who, by order of Major Paterson at Moascar, was not allowed to be mounted. By chance, the depot officer explained, the trainer mistakenly saddled up Bill, not William. As it was only the commander-in-chief's pride that had been hurt and nothing else, the trainer was fired from the Jericho depot and sent back to Moascar for disciplinary action there.

'You've made a terrible mistake, Private Hickey,' Paterson said, his face expressionless, when the wiry, redheaded trainer, accompanied by Sutherland, entered his office at Moascar. 'There could have been an awful accident, with Bloody Bull!'

'But there wasn't, Major,' Hickey remarked. 'General Chauvel saved the day.'

'Hmm. But Bloody Bull was badly shaken, I hear?'

'I wasn't there but, yes, I heard he was all shook up, sir.'

'I must discipline you, Private,' Paterson said. 'You must take a week off in Cairo. You'll need a depot car.'

'Will my pay be docked, Major?'

'Don't think that will be necessary, but you will need expenses. Cairo's best hotels and whorehouses are costly these days.'

23

THE OPPORTUNIST

Charlotte cooled in her appreciation of Shanahan after her sisters' hostility, but he kept bringing her gifts.

'My God!' she exclaimed one day at lunchtime when she unwrapped a gift of a stylish bottle of La Passionata. 'This is my favourite perfume. I've never been able to afford it.'

Shanahan played with his walking sticks, not making eye contact.

'How did you know?' she asked.

'What?'

'That it was my favourite?'

'I . . . um . . . I like it. I find it alluring. So I wanted you to wear it.'

She scrutinised him.

'What?' he asked, looking up to meet her gaze.

'C'mon, which girlfriend of yours wore it?'

'I got it at that special apothecary in Piccadilly, the one near Simpson's. The assistant showed me a few samples.' She looked sceptical as he added, 'You know, they make their own perfumes and sell a few imported ones. I liked this best. It's from Paris.'

'You went to that trouble . . .?' she said softly. 'So thoughtful. Thank you.' She kissed him. 'Stanley wouldn't . . .' Charlotte checked herself.

'Stanley wouldn't what?'

'Oh, nothing,' she said with a pensive expression.

'Don't tell me he bought you this?'

'No,' she said, almost inaudibly, 'no, he didn't.'

Shanahan never missed bringing her flowers when they went out, and never the same kind, except for red roses, which he gave her twice. He began asking her out to music hall shows, which they both loved. He would get tickets for performances at Hoxton Street, the London Empire on High Street, Shoreditch, at Collins' on Islington Green and his favourite venue, the Olympia Music Hall. Charlotte quickly realised that Shanahan was a very active individual who had overcome his disability with verve and a zest for life that she had not experienced before. He handled his two sticks with such skill that he could keep up with anyone while walking with just a slight limp. He kept fit with an exercise regime to put an Olympian to shame and always seemed to have energy to spare.

After watching a production of *The Merry Widow* at Leicester Square in London's West End, they walked into an alley where he had left his motorbike. Three young toughs were taking turns trying to start it.

Shanahan hustled down to them, leaving Charlotte looking concerned.

'Hey,' he growled, 'get off that bike!'

One of them jumped into the sidecar, bouncing it up and down.

'Get off!' Shanahan said as he reached them.

'Huh, peg-leg!' one jeered. 'What are you goin' to do abart it, hey?'

Shanahan didn't answer. He balanced his left side with the two sticks and threw a sharp punch at the jaw of the one on the sidecar. The youth fell with a groan and his head bounced on the cobblestones. Another one gesticulated as if he would retaliate. Shanahan swung one of his sticks hard into the second youth's rib-cage, knocking the air from his lungs and causing him to slump to his knees in pain. The third 'tough' helped his mates to their feet and the three staggered off down the alley. Seconds later, Charlotte reached him. He examined the sidecar.

'It's a bit loose,' he said, 'you better hop on behind me. I'll fix it when we get home.'

'My God!' she said as she straddled the seat and placed her arms around his chest to hold on. 'You really threw a punch there. That fool will be sore tonight.'

'I used to box,' he said, and added softly as they sped off, 'haven't got the footwork these days.'

The next weekend, Shanahan invited her a second time to join him for a drive down to Hove near Brighton.

Charlotte hesitated. Stanley Butler was going grouse-hunting in Scotland again but she was unsure about spending a Saturday night with another man.

'We can take two rooms at a nice guesthouse,' Shanahan said, anticipating her concern.

'You're so sweet to me,' she said, squeezing his arm, 'so understanding.'

After leaving their bags at the guesthouse, they decided to dine early near Brighton Pier at a cafe overlooking the water. They had just walked in the cafe door when Charlotte went white and her hand went to her mouth. His eyes settled on a good-looking, tall man with a moustache sitting opposite a shapely young brunette. They seemed intimate. Charlotte turned and walked out.

'Take me home!' she demanded as she slipped into the sidecar and buried her head in her hands. Shanahan drove along the beach road. There was a cool breeze. People were promenading. Shanahan looked back. Charlotte was sobbing gently. He pulled the bike over and parked it outside a fish and chip shop.

'C'mon, girl,' he said, helping her out, 'let's eat.'

'I'm not hungry,' she snapped.

'I am,' he said, leading her into the shop. He called a waiter over and helped her choose a meal. She hardly said a word for five minutes.

'It was Stanley, wasn't it?' he asked.

'Why did he lie?'

'Funny-looking grouse,' he said.

'What?' she said, looking up. Then she scowled. 'Very funny! Not now, Michael, please!'

Shanahan convinced her to stay at the guesthouse. He was asleep in his room when he was woken by the door opening. Charlotte entered and slipped into the bed beside him. She hugged him. He eased himself over to face her.

'Ever made love to a one-legged man before?' he asked, drawing a gentle smile from her.

'No,' she whispered, and added coyly, 'I've never made love to anybody . . .'

*

Charlotte confronted her fiancé Stanley Butler a day later. He confessed to an affair with a secretary and Charlotte called off the relationship.

Shanahan saw his opportunity. He invited Charlotte to dinner at Scott's, an upmarket West End restaurant, and proposed. He had borrowed money and bought a smart diamond engagement ring. Charlotte was stunned. She knew he was 'keen' but because of his laconic manner, she had not been sure how much he appreciated her. Now she knew.

After recovering from the shock, she asked for time to think about it.

'No, no time,' he said. 'I want an answer right now, tonight.' Seeing her bewilderment, he added, '. . . or tomorrow, or next week. In fact, whenever you feel inclined to say yes.'

She laughed. He plied her with wine. After several drinks, she said: 'You know, I'm twenty-seven next month. Almost an old maid! Not getting any younger.'

'Wish I could use that line,' Shanahan said. She wasn't sure if he was being funny or frank, but she giggled anyway.

'Bloody Australia!' she said. 'I'm going to join the convicts.'

'I take that as a "yes",' he said, reaching for her hand.

24

THE RUSE

Harry Chauvel, who had been knighted and promoted to lieutenant-general, devised a shrewd plan to fool the Turks before the last important thrust to drive them from Palestine, Syria and Arabia. The secret aim was to move his Light Horse force west to the coast at Jaffa where they would be hidden in orange groves. They would wait for the British infantry to make a shock attack and punch a hole in the Turkish defence forces in Palestine's north. Then the horsemen would emerge from the orange groves, thrust through the gap in the Turkish lines and ride north. The aim would be to defeat the one enemy army there before sweeping east to take on the second enemy army in Palestine. After that it planned to ride further east and north to tackle the third Turkish

229

army, which was being harassed by Lawrence's Arabs in Jordan.

Chauvel had to make the Turks believe his force would be staying in the Jordan Valley. It was September 1918. His 34,000 horsemen and cavalry would have to succeed, otherwise, when the war ended, the Turks might still be in Palestine, Syria, Jordan and Arabia, which would mean they would retain that territory in a carve-up following an armistice. In effect, the Turks would maintain their dominance in the Middle East, as they had done since the sixteenth century, making the past three years' effort by the British amount to securing just the Sinai and acquiring southern Palestine.

Part of Chauvel's ruse was to stage a five-event race meeting near Jericho, not far from the Turkish defences on the Jordan River. The Turks' scouts and spies would be able to see the build-up to the event. A program was to be printed and distributed in all major towns, and primarily Jerusalem, to make sure that the Turks knew about it.

Chauvel called a meeting at his Jericho HQ days before secretly driving to his HQ at the village of Sarona, five kilometres north of Jaffa on the coast, where he would oversee the build-up of horsemen.

'The main event should be billed as a Melbourne-Cup style race,' he told several select officers, 'but we can't call it that. It won't be a handicap event.'

'How about a cross been Palestine and Melbourne,' one officer suggested, 'the *Palbourne* Cup?'

Chauvel winced. 'Bit insipid and obscure,' he replied, 'need a bit of alliteration. Something like "The Cairo Cup".'

'The Jericho Cup?' a second officer proffered.

'That's better. It has a sweet ring to it. That name also lets the Turks know where it is.'

The Jericho Cup was adopted.

'And the length?' Chauvel asked. 'Must be at least two miles.'

'Longer,' another officer suggested. 'That will mean we can use leaflets saying that the biggest and strongest Walers in the entire force will be tested in the race. Hopefully this will make the enemy believe the authenticity of the event. The Turks would know that our eighty strongest horses would always be in the front line of any attack. If they think they are racing in the east, clearly we could not be planning anything in the west.'

'Let's make it three miles then,' Chauvel decided. 'Make sure the horses are not watered for, say, twenty-four hours before the event. That will mean they will go harder when they get wind of the well as they head into the straight.'

'General Allenby has asked that Major Paterson's big Arabian thoroughbreds be in the event. They would not be in any attack, so that helps.'

'It would be good to have Bill the Bastard up against them,' a third officer commented.

Chauvel nodded. 'I saw him do the despatch run at Gallipoli. He was strong and covered more than three miles speedily enough. But no one can ride him, except that Aborigine . . . what's his name, Mullagh?'

'He hasn't stayed on him for very long,' the third officer remarked. 'Besides, Major Paterson ordered him not to be used as other than a packhorse, out of respect for his efforts at Romani.'

'That directive applied only to battle,' Chauvel corrected, 'I don't think it matters if he is in a race.'

'But could Mullagh last three or four minutes on him?' the first officer asked.

'Only one way to find out,' Chauvel said.

*

More than 10,000 spectators—including 5000 British infantry and Indian soldiers, about 1000 Anzacs not required in Jaffa, and 4000 bribed locals—lined the rough dirt and sand track just outside Jericho. The crowd's size gave the meeting an authenticity. Turks guarding their camps on the Jordan River used binoculars to see the build-up of the spectators. The event promised to be gruelling in the projected 90-degree Fahrenheit temperature in early autumn.

Betting was rife, especially among the Anzacs, and some sizeable wagers were laid out with bookies from as far away as Cairo. Many Light Horsemen, stealthily tucked away at Jaffa and waiting for the order to attack, put money on the Jericho Cup.

The fifth and final race on the program had fifteen starters. The non-Walers were the big Arabian horses owned by Paterson, including Khartoum, Tut 1, Tut 2 and Blackham. Jackie Mullagh agreed to ride Bill the

Bastard. Most of the alleged 'smart' money was on the powerful black stallion Khartoum. He had the fastest times by far over the Melbourne Cup distance of two miles and had been clocked and trained over this distance for two years. The next best times had been scored, in order, by Blackham the white mare, Tut 1 the gelding and Tut 2 the stallion. Two stayers from South Africa had been able to clock faster times than the remaining nine starters. Bill had never been timed with a jockey on him and the only guide was his Gallipoli despatch run, but that had been without a rider for most of the distance.

The Jericho Cup was not a handicap race so Khartoum, who carried an ex-professional Sydney jockey, was the out and out favourite. By the beginning of the event punters could not put a bet on him. Bookies, some experienced operators from Melbourne and Sydney, had never seen such a huge plunge in percentage terms compared to other competitors. There was one bet of 750 pounds from Cairo, and the bookies suspected a former owner of Khartoum in play. Some wagers were around 50 quid, a year's income for a serviceman.

Some spectators wandered close to the 'track', which was a crescent shape running the three miles. Most in the crowd wore headgear to protect them from the sun and sat on sand mounds around the course. Some found meagre shade from palms at the only oasis, where a well dispensed water about fifty metres beyond the finish line. A make-shift horse trough was set up for the thirsty competitors after they reached the line.

The first four races were largely non-events. Some horses gave up before the end of the mile races, others crashed into each other. Two went lame struggling over the sand and had to be shot. One was bitten by a scorpion and had to be retired for treatment while another poor mare appeared to have been bitten by an asp and collapsed. A trooper arrived with a rifle to put it down but the animal died before he could take aim.

The crowd seemed listless and disinterested, except for the Anzacs, who were betting on every race. Against orders, many of the troopers had alcohol and were becoming boisterous, then obstreperous, in the trying heat. Fights broke out. Military police waded into the crowd near the finishing post and made a dozen arrests.

Meanwhile Paterson sat in his office at Moascar with about forty trainers crowded around a cable machine which would send a placings report for each minute of the Jericho Cup. At Jaffa, hundreds of troopers hovered near the officers' HQ waiting for word on the first three place-getters.

At 6 pm in the Jordan Valley the heat had been taken out of the day and the humidity was at its lowest. The fifteen starters in the Jericho Cup variously sauntered, trotted, pranced and cantered to the start line. There were no stalls, just a taut rope across the track which would be dropped when signalled by the starter's revolver.

Mullagh was the only jockey to ride bareback. In the scores of truncated rides he had had on Bill, he found this was the best way to go. He was also the only rider not to mount up on the way to the start line. An officer acting as the chief steward asked him why he had not done so.

'I can't risk it,' Mullagh said, clearly suffering from nerves. 'I don't want him to bolt before the race begins.'

Mullagh had walked Bill for an hour at dawn. He had taken him for a nailbiting short run of about a furlong before a long drink and a further relaxing walk. His lungs were opened. While the other races were on Mullagh had walked him a third time and had risked another ride, a quick second furlong dash.

One writer to record the event was the author and cricket specialist A Sumner Reed, who had covered the Melbourne races when a junior reporter at the *Herald*. He was a member of the brigade's brass band, which had struck up before each race. After drumming in the earlier events, the balding 50-year-old Anglo-Australian retired to write a full report on the event. He positioned himself on horseback halfway around the course and took notes, which he would have typed up for posterity. He, like all the other onlookers, had no idea that the race was part of a ruse to fool the Turks into a false sense of security.

Reed was intrigued by all the impressive thorough-breds but planned to watch Bill the Bastard with particular interest. He had seen quite big side-bets put on the distance that the big Waler would travel before he removed his jockey. Most picked the first half-mile for Mullagh's dislodgement.

Just before the betting books were closed at 6 pm a gentle plunge was placed from Jaffa by Chook Mulherin, who put ten pounds on Bill at 50 to 1. He had placed the bet ten hours earlier in a cable despatch to Jericho HQ and it had just reached the bookie concerned.

The bookie with a booming voice laughed at the bet. 'This is the second bet I've taken for the Bastard to finish the race with the jockey still on 'im!' he roared to a fellow bookie a few yards away. 'The rest are on where he will buck his rider off, with the exception bein' the bloody jockey himself! Mullagh put a fiver on. Felt sorry for him and gave him 50 to 1.'

'Is he allowed to bet on himself?'

'Only if he reckons he'll stay on.'

They both laughed.

The stewards began to line up the horses as best they could.

'Get on him or I'll disqualify him,' the chief steward ordered Mullagh.

In between exercises, Bill had been quite gentle all day but that meant nothing with his mercurial character. Mullagh kept one eye on Khartoum, knowing that these two had a 'history'. The big black stallion was near the 'fence', or left of the track. Mullagh took Bill to the far side, where no other jockey wanted to be. Then he took a breath and mounted him. Bill remained impassive. Mullagh patted him.

Bill wandered up to the line. Ringing in Mullagh's ears were Shanahan's words of advice two years earlier: 'Show Bill respect all the time and he will give it back, *most* of the time . . . Never hit him or yell at him. Keep a long rein. Don't jerk him ever, but be firm. Let him know what you want. If he is feeling good, he will do some if not all of what you want . . . Never dig a stirrup into him. Use a gentle heel. Heel and hands, that's what he responds to. Sweet words of praise in his ear never hurt. He knows your voice. Stroke his mane. You must have an inner rapport with Bill . . . He has to believe in you . . . Remember, this animal is the smartest four-legged anything that you will ever meet . . . Respect his intelligence . . . Embrace it and give it a chance to breathe and create . . .'

Mullagh looked along the line-up and noticed he was the only rider without a whip. The starter's gun fired and the horses began raggedly. Mullagh used a feather-touch of his hand on Bill, who responded by building slowly from a light gallop to something resembling an interest in being in touch with the field. Khartoum blazed to the lead early, followed by Tut 1 and Blackham. Tut 2 was in a difficult mood and well back in the field after the first two furlongs.

Mullagh kept up an encouraging chat in Bill's ear but tried not to sound too urgent. He lifted himself off the horse's back to give Bill some sense of freedom from his rider. Mullagh recalled Shanahan telling him: 'He is used to me and he accepts my weight, my presence. But if you are on him, try to make it seem as if you are not on him, like a jockey. It will help.'

Bill was running second last as they passed the rough first mile post marked by two palm trees near a disused well. Mullagh kept his head down, only looking up to see how far behind he was. All the horses were finding the going tough. The track was 'heavy', not from rain but the occasional thick layers of sand that made it a plough for every runner. Bill was pulling through well but his pace was slow. At a mile and two furlongs he was neck and neck for last place. The next furlong was very slow, even for the front runner Khartoum, who was forty metres in front of Tut 1 and Blackham, fighting out second place. The sand was deep and soft. All the horses pushed hard. The whips were out everywhere.

A Sumner Reed had positioned himself high on a sand-hill at the halfway mark. He could see the complete field. He used binoculars to watch Bill and noticed that Mullagh was stroking his neck all through the tough plough of that stretch. Bill was pulling harder than any horse. He pounded past six competitors and was running eighth when they all emerged onto red dirt. Reed saw something else from his vantage point. Bill was the only horse moving at pace. He was making up ground on the middle bunch. Reed pushed his horse down the slope and was galloping ahead of the front runners on a flat stretch next to the track. He reached the two mile point and looked back. Khartoum had stretched his lead to fifty metres but, like all the runners, he was struggling. He had done his training length run of the Melbourne Cup and seemed to be slackening off. His jockey was using the whip so much that the horse seemed distracted. The same applied to Tut 1 and Tut 2, who were gaining on the leader. The rider on Blackham was the only one not using the whip apart from Mullagh. Reed stopped to take notes. He scribbled 'Bill, Fifth—one mile to go'. He watched as Bill grunted past, his nostrils flaring and pulling in the oxygen for his big lungs. Mullagh was hanging on, his derriere well above Bill's back. Reed galloped on but could not keep pace with the front runners.

At two miles and a furlong, Khartoum was being challenged by Tut 2, who had settled down and was running on better than the others.

Mullagh felt in harmony with Bill for the first time in perhaps all their rides. The race had now been going for more than three minutes and Bill had not attempted even a playful buck. He seemed to be concentrating on what was ahead. At two-and-a-half miles, Bill was still running fifth. He could smell the water. Mullagh had given him a fair drink in the morning, although this had been against the race guidelines, which had suggested that a horse would run better without water for a day.

At two miles, five furlongs the front runners had bunched. Khartoum was still in the lead but by only two lengths, with Blackham second, Tut 2 third and Tut 1 fourth. Bill was a further three lengths behind, but Reed reckoned Bill had moved faster than any horse over the past mile. His tremendous strength was beginning to tell.

Half the spectators were bunched around the finishing tape three furlongs away. Their animated cheering could be heard floating over the thick evening air. Two furlongs from the finish, Blackham and Khartoum were neck and neck. Blackham's jockey was using the whip for the first time. Bill had caught Tut 1 and Tut 2. Mullagh felt a thrill up his spine as he realised Bill was actually trying to pace and beat the others, something not evident in the race until this moment. Bill was being his unpredictable self. One furlong out, the desert evening air carried the roar as Bill burnt off Tut 1 and Tut 2. Mullagh was too nervous to urge him on overly hard for fear of a sudden turn-off, but he heard himself say close to Bill's ear: 'C'*mon*, Bill you Bastard! You can take that big black bugger!'

Khartoum had Blackham beaten 110 metres from the line. Bill moved up and took the game mare too. Khartoum was now only a length in front. Bill moved up close. They were neck and neck as the tape came into view. Bill swerved close and the move seemed to startle Khartoum, who may have had memories of Bill's attack three years earlier. Fifty metres from the line, Bill's head was down, his tail straight out. Mullagh now was just riding him without any control at all. Bill edged half a length in front at the tape.

The cheering was more for the excitement of the competitive finish than the joy of anyone backing a winner. Hundreds of spectators looked on in disbelief as Bill, Khartoum and the others thundered by and were directed towards the water trough. Mullagh tried to pull Bill up but he charged past the trough and straight up a high sand dune. He reached the crest and stopped, sweating and snorting. Mullagh could feel the horse's mighty heart pounding. He expected Bill to attempt to throw him, but instead he stood pawing the sand and settling himself after such an effort. Mullagh waited for a minute. Bill walked along the crest, as if in triumph at his feat. Mullagh eased him down the slope. Close to the trough, Mullagh relaxed, but just as he did, Bill reared up, catching his jockey by surprise. Mullagh was thrown off. He landed awkwardly, twisting his ankle. It brought a roar of laughter from the onlookers near the trough. Mullagh hobbled about cursing and then limped up to Bill.

'You just had to show me who was boss, didn't you?' Mullagh said as he led Bill to the water. A swarm of spectators congratulated Mullagh. He kept patting Bill as he drank.

'It wasn't me,' he repeated to well-wishers, 'it was Bill. He ran his own race. I was only there for the ride.'

The crowd admired his modesty, even though Mullagh protested that he meant what he said. Seconds later, he received a surprise when the bookie with whom he had placed the bet sidled up beside him. He shook hands with Mullagh, who felt a rolled-up envelope being pushed into his palm. It contained 250 pounds.

'Put that in your pocket and don't say nothin' to no one, young man,' the bookie said out of the corner of his mouth. Mullagh digested the emphatic triple negative and pocketed the money.

A hundred kilometres west on the coast at Sarona HQ, a cable operator confirmed the placings: 1, Bill the Bastard; 2, Khartoum; 3, Blackham; and 4, Tut 2.

'I've won five hundred quid!' Mulherin said to Legg as they wandered back to their camp in the groves. 'That big, beautiful neddie!'

'Jeez! That's enough to buy a couple of good bush properties back home,' Legg said.

'I'm going to kiss Mullagh when I see him! How did he bloody well do it?'

'Kiss the major too,' Legg said. 'He taught Mullagh how to handle Bill.'

'And you can kiss Bill for me!'

They reached their tents as night fell and were greeted by a major.

'Get some rest, you blokes,' he said. 'We are moving out after midnight.'

*

Chauvel's ruse had worked. The Turks believed that the cavalry/Light Horse thrust would be in the east and not the west. Captured enemy intelligence maps as late as 10 am on 18 September, the day of the Jericho Cup meeting, showed that the Australian mounted division and British cavalry were still thought to be at the base in Jericho, close to where the Cup race was held.

Learning this, Chauvel decided now was the time to strike.

Darkness turned the lazy countryside east of Jaffa into a seething mass of movement under moonlit skies. The artillery, cars, men, horses, camels and mules brought up to the front in the last few hours jammed every thoroughfare going north. Silence was imposed, although the creaking of wagons, purr of lorries, crunch of boots on metallic roads and the odd groan of the camels and whinnying of the horses could not be avoided.

The moon set at 4 am on 19 September 1918 as British troops made their last-minute adjustments to weapons and gear. A half-hour later they attacked on a thirteen-kilometre front in from the coast and confronted the Turks less than two kilometres away. They breached enemy lines and the cavalry and Light Horse rode through the gap.

Chauvel's force galloped eighty kilometres on 19 September and took a key Turkish communications centre and rail junction at El Afule. He just missed capturing the senior German commander Liman von Sanders, who had been behind the Turkish stand at Gallipoli and was now running the two Turkish armies in Palestine. He escaped the town of Nazareth in his pyjamas, chauffeured out in a Mercedes.

The Turks were in disarray and on the run north-west with Chauvel's horsemen in hot pursuit.

25

AN HONOUR FOR THE 10TH REGIMENT

Shanahan was pleased to receive a letter from Mulherin, for more reasons than one. It told him of Bill's ride and win with Mullagh as his jockey, and an envelope within the letter contained a hundred pounds. Mulherin wrote:

If you hadn't trained the Bastard and Mullagh, they would never have won the Cup. I backed them and won big. Wanted to give you a little gift in appreciation and knowing that you'll be strapped for cash with that baby on the way—when is it, next month? Also I wanted to tell you another whisper about your little mate Bill. He has become quite a legend in his own hay-loft. We've learnt tonight (27 September) that he has been seconded for a special assignment, as a packhorse, I hasten to add, not a battle-neddie. Harry Chauvel is rumoured to have selected the West's 10th Regiment to take Damascus any day now. There is something big in his decision. He wanted to send either the 10th or the Vics' 8th because of them being deci- mated on Gallipoli. He ordained that one of them should have the chance at ultimate glory. You've got to admit General Harry cares about us, and history! We hear the two regiments drew straws. The 10th got it. Their 2IC, a Perth dentist, Arthur Olden, will command the attack. I've met him. He is a real character! Some reckon he is as mad as a hatter, and he agrees with them! No one knows if he is joking or not! He tells everybody that all dentists go mad eventually because they use mercury in dental fillings. He says hatters were called 'mad' because they used mercury blocks to shape top hats! At the very least the mercury tale is a cunning excuse for his eccentricity. Olden is taking quite a big force—400 troopers—on the Damascus assignment. He must be thinking they'll be doing some very big looting! Hence the biggest pack-animals, although this does not explain why his requisition sheet specifically asks for 'Bill the Bastard'. Anyway Bill has left the depot. He would be somewhere south of Damascus as I write . . .

The neat, trim Captain Arthur Olden rallied his troopers before dawn on 1 October 1918 and they prepared for what all believed could be the ride of their lives. Most had had little sleep while fellow Anzac troopers high in the mountains of the Barada Gorge fired down on some 4000 Turks and Germans who were trying to escape through the narrow gorge passageway from Damascus west to Beirut. The German commanders would not let their Turkish counterparts surrender. Instead of receiving mercy for giving up, they were met with a shower of bullets from the Australians. Every enemy soldier was killed.

The noise through the night was hideous, but the resting Light Horsemen preparing for the attack on Damascus were used to it. Many of Olden's 10th Regiment were hardened warriors who had survived Gallipoli and come on the long ride from Cairo to claim revenge against the Turks. This had taken four years. Sleep or no sleep, they were not going to miss what was ahead. They did not expect the easy 'kangaroo shoot', as the previous night's trooper marksmen characterised the ease of hitting the enemy trying to escape through the gorge. For one thing, there were 20,000 Turks holed up in two garrisons, one in Damascus and the other across the river on the approach to the city. They were rumoured to be out of food and ammunition, but no one could be sure. Besides, they were Mustafa Kemal's troops. He and they had been unforgiving at Gallipoli. To expect anything less this time would be folly and could end in disaster.

Olden had his troopers, plus twenty packhorses and mules headed by Bill, line up for the 30-kilometre ride into the unknown, with one secret intention in mind. Allenby had issued strict orders that no British (meaning Anzac Light Horse) troops were to enter Damascus itself, but every artery from it had to be cut off. The reason for this directive from the commander-in-chief was not explained to Chauvel. It had been given to allow Lawrence and his Arab army into Damascus first. In other words, Olden was expected to secure the city so that Lawrence and his Arabs could march in and claim they had liberated and taken the Syrian capital. There was a delicious piece of British double-dealing in this. The French had been promised Syria in the British–French carve-up of the Middle East after the Turks had been forced out (the so-called Sykes–Picot agreement of 1916), but at the last minute the British had decided to make it *seem* as if the Arabs had won Damascus. The Arabs in turn would say that they wished the British, and not the French, to share the spoils of Syria with them. If the Light Horse attacked the town and took it, this would ruin the British–Arab game.

When Chauvel directed Olden to secure the town, he told him: 'You are to cut off the Turks and keep them bottled up in the city. The C-'n'-C has directed that on no account are you to enter the city. However, clearly, if there is no way to cut off the northern exit, you will have to go *through* Damascus to reach it. If you go through the city, you may encounter resistance. In that case you may have to change your plans. You may even have to fight the Turks and secure the surrender of the city. Do you understand, Captain?'

'Yes, General,' Olden said with a straight face and thoughtful stroke of his clipped moustache. 'You want the Light Horse to take Damascus.'

'Very good, Captain. But you never received that command from me.'

'Of course not, General,' Olden said with a wry look before he frowned and asked: 'What about this Lawrence fellow and the Arabs? We hear rumours that Allenby wants them to appear to "conquer" Damascus. Our journalists are being ordered to report events that way.'

'Off the record, Captain, that will not happen. The Arabs will not risk the possibility of confronting 20,000 Turks, no matter what their rumoured state of disrepair.'

'No, you're right, General. They prefer hit and run tactics. They never charge, at least in big numbers.'

'The Arabs will wait and see what happens to you, Captain, when you and your troopers try to cut off all the arteries into the city.'

Olden's face creased into a smile. 'My boys will relish the opportunity, General, I can assure you of that. Some of them have come all the way from the Nek for this moment. We all have long memories.'

'That's why the 10th have been given the moment, Captain.'

He shook hands with Olden and added: 'I know you'll seize it.'

*

The regiment began its advance by descending the steep mountains to the Barada River where they watered the horses. Olden trotted up and down the line and noticed that one horse was not drinking.

'Sergeant!' he bellowed. 'Why is that one not at the river?'

'That's Bill the Bastard, Captain.'

'I know who it is. Why isn't he being watered?'

'He doesn't want to drink. No one can make him. Believe me, Captain, we have all tried to get him there.'

Olden trotted away and returned a minute later.

'Sergeant, take all Bill's packs off him and distribute them with the mules. Then bring Bill up to the head of the column. Saddle him up, reverse the stirrups and put a spare pair of boots in 'em.'

This seemed a quirky request, but all the officers and NCOs were trained to expect the unexpected from Olden. And they knew he studied military history obsessively.

'Excuse me, Captain, but doesn't that represent a fallen general or somethin' at a funeral?'

'Not what I have in mind, Sergeant. Genghis Khan began the practice when he wanted a horse sacrificed to serve his fallen warrior in the next world.' He patted Bill. 'But we are using it differently, more in the later tradition of the caparisoned horse symbolic of a warrior who will ride no more.'

The order was carried out. All the horses were nearly watered. Bill was delivered to the head of the column lining up behind Olden.

'Can you guess why Bill is at the front?' Olden asked a lieutenant.

'You want to mount him, Captain?'

The other lieutenants laughed.

'Good God no! I'd rather remove a tiger's tooth without a tranquilliser.'

'There are 12,000 Turks in the first garrison, Lieutenant. If we have to go down the road and cross the river to engage them, what is the first thing they will see?'

The lieutenant nodded understandingly. 'They will see us being led by the most powerful charging horse,' he replied, 'but riderless with stirrups reversed.'

'Exactly. It will put the wind up 'em, Lieutenant.'

'But what will they think of him riderless? Would the Turks understand the tradition?'

'Don't know, but like you, Lieutenant, they will be confused, and that is what we want in our enemy. *Confusion*.' He reached across and stroked Bill's mane. 'Tell the sergeant to pass the word down the line,' he said, 'Bill the Bastard is symbolic of all our fallen cobbers from the Nek and elsewhere. They are gone to God, but they are with us today!'

Olden looked back along his column as the sergeant carried out the instruction. Many troopers reacted with a yell and raised fist. After a few minutes Olden held up his right hand.

'Forward!' he called.

*

They crossed the river and headed for the Dumar station where a train had drawn up. The horsemen of the lead squadron drew their swords and charged around a bend in the road. Some 800 Turkish soldiers were bunched in a disorderly fashion ready to board the train that would be escaping west to Beirut. When they saw Bill and the lead horsemen thundering in their direction, many raised their hands high. Olden called for their surrender, along with another 200 Turks on board. He turned to one of his officers.

'Quite a haul here,' he said and, pointing to the large batch of new prisoners, added: 'Select a troop and look after this mob. But don't march 'em off yet. I want to see what's on this train.'

Another troop of thirty-two boarded the train and moved through each carriage. They found a storage compartment with four chests and a dozen boxes. One of the chests was jemmied open.

'Ooh!' a sergeant said, wide-eyed. 'Better call the captain in.' Olden boarded the train and was shown the chest. It was filled with gold and silver coins.

'Ah, me hearties,' Olden exclaimed, 'what do we have here? Treasure! Wonderful! I can see this melted down for a million tooth fillings.' He ordered the chests taken from the train. 'You'll need a truck for this lot.'

Olden cut open the boxes himself.

'Cigars!' He smiled. 'And good German ones too.' He ran one past his nose. 'Great aroma!' He had them quickly distributed to every trooper. Olden opened other boxes and found bottles of cognac.

'Goodness me!' Olden said, using a knife to lift the top off a bottle. Enticing fumes wafted out. He sampled a swig of the cognac and handed it around, saying: 'Very smooth. The German commanders did live well in Damascus.'

'There is quite a lot of other loot, Captain,' a sergeant said. 'Should we use the packhorses to take it to the base?'

'No way, Sergeant,' Olden said. 'I won't have Bill and his cobbers used for such mundane activity. See if you can acquire another truck. No, better still, get our Turkish contingent here to carry their own stuff. But not the gold, silver, cognac or the rest of the cigars. They must be trucked.'

Olden ordered his force to mount up. 'Pass it down the line,' he said to a lieutenant, 'I want every trooper who smokes to light up when we hit the run into Damascus. Will give us a very classy look!'

Olden leant across to Bill, offering him a cigar. The horse sniffed and rejected it.

'Only smoke carrots, eh, Bill? Smart horse.'

Soon the force, minus the guard troop, was riding off. Fifteen minutes later they were blocked on the road at the bottom of the gorge by the destruction caused by their fellow troopers' brutal blockade in the night. Human and animal bodies and broken transport littered the way. Olden ordered a work detail to clear the path. He and his officers watched the grisly business as dead Germans and Turks were piled up.

'Show a bit of respect, boys!' Olden called out to the detail. 'Line up the bodies in rows. They will be buried later.' Olden noticed that his men were sobered by what they were seeing as the detail worked. He guessed that many were thinking that these victims could be them if things went wrong in the next few hours. He thought he should lighten the moment.

He waited until the detail had finished its job then addressed a sergeant with all his officers listening: 'You heard about Napoleon, who asked his dresser to bring him his red shirt when he saw an enemy army coming to a hill-top opposite?' The others waited. They all loved Olden's humour. 'His dresser asked why he wanted his red shirt. Napoleon said, "Because when I am wounded my men will not know it". His dresser asked if he wanted his red trousers too. Napoleon thought that would be a good idea. Just then he looked up to see another three enemy armies appearing on other hill-tops. He said to his dresser: "Better still, bring me my brown trousers".'

The listeners laughed and it seemed to take the tension out of the moment. Seconds later he held up his cigar and commanded: 'Light up!'

The troopers lit cigars. Olden motioned again for them to ride out.

The long column built quickly to a gallop, which created a swirl of cigar smoke above them and another of dust below them. They took the first turn out of the gorge and soon could see the tips of Damascus's minarets, sparkling in the day's first light. They were on the direct road to the city and its spread of green gardens made even more colourful by flowering fruit trees. The sweet aroma of jasmine and the whiff of citrus flowers in the cool orchards were sharp and pleasant in the crisp autumn air, providing a contrast to the heady pungency of the cigars.

Bill pounded along in front, pulling the rope connecting him to a minding trooper.

'He's setting a hot pace!' the trooper called loudly so he could be heard above the rumble of hooves. 'Must think he's in another bloody Jericho Cup!'

The gorge was on the left. On the right was the river and the railway, separated from the road by a high stone wall. Military barracks came into view about 500 metres away across the river. A big body of Turkish troops inside the compound could be seen from the troopers' elevated position. Some Turks hastened to the walls with rifles, others could be seen running inside the building. Olden lifted his binoculars.

'They look a very sorry lot,' he said. 'Watch 'em, boys. Remember they belong to Mustafa Kemal. If the bugger is there, they will fight.' He lowered his glasses. 'We'll soon find out.'

They galloped on. A bridge was ahead.

'Do we cross the river, Captain?' a lieutenant asked.

'Not unless they fire at us.'

'They're lifting their rifles!' a lieutenant called.

'Swords drawn!' Olden yelled. With that, about 370 weapons glinted in the sunlight as they were unsheathed from scabbards. No shots were fired. The troopers rode past the bridge. Olden pulled out in front and held his sword aloft. He built the pace to a fast gallop, creating a shroud of dust and a rumble that was heard in the city. Citizens wandered to the main artery's entrance gate to see the troopers thundering their way.

'The British are coming!' an Arab yelled, and the cry was repeated again and again, drawing more curious onlookers. Crowds built up in the streets. They had been waiting all night for this moment when they expected to be liberated from their long-time Turkish masters.

Olden slowed the column as they approached the open gates to the city.

'Keep column formation!' he ordered at the top of his voice.

There was no hostility, no resistance. Instead, they were surrounded by well-wishers. Women threw garlands from windows. Men offered them drinks, fruit and other food. There were gasps at the sight of the Light Horse, and Bill drew the most awed expressions. The Walers were fitter and larger than their own horses, and Bill would have seemed like a giant. Despite the excitement, he remained calm until one exuberant young Arab tried to mount him. Bill reacted by lifting his front half high. The Arab slid back hard onto the cobblestones and limped away, wincing in pain, much to the amusement of the mob. Onlookers now backed away from Bill and created a path forward.

Some in the crowd revealed their allegiances. There were rugged mountain Arabs—the Druse—who had filtered in at night over the last week from the distant Hauran mountains, uniformed gendarmerie, European-suited Syrians, Jews, Greeks, Armenians, and even some Turkish civilians. They were all excited. Rifles were fired into the air. The troopers reached for revolvers. Some horses reared up. The Anzacs soon realised the shooters were not hostile, but it unsettled them. How were they to know the difference? Snipers were rife when they entered cities. Many a trooper and horse had been killed this way.

The column followed the road onto the bridge that crossed the Barada River near the Victoria Hotel. The throng surged close. Bill was next to a big trooper on a Waler nearly as tall as Bill. The two horses forced a passage. Another foolhardy Arab tried to slip a garland over Bill's head. The horse reared up and shook it off, scaring the crowd. The Australians and their mounts were in no mood to acknowledge the men and women who continued to press their appreciation on them. The troopers were alert and grim. They had not expected a festival. Nor had they expected the enemy to have fled or to be impotent.

They made a path through the crowded streets to the Town Hall. The steps were busy with officials and well-dressed locals. It was not yet 6.30 am but the place was alive. Olden halted his column. He used an interpreter to discover that the governor of Damascus and Syria was waiting for them in the hall. Olden and three lieutenants dismounted and drew revolvers, leaving five riderless mounts at the front of the column. This was an invitation to more young Arabs to try to jump on them. Olden turned and fired his revolvers over their heads. The pranksters backed off. He led his men up the steps and along corridors, guided by officials.

They were met by Emir Said, the man who had been left by the Turks as the nominal governor. Olden took the moment to demand the surrender of the city, which was duly accepted. He called for the surrender to be written out. Documents were signed. Olden was impatient. He ordered that the local gendarmerie keep order and prevent looting. Mindful of the fact that the bulk of the Turkish army was escaping, he wished to continue his pursuit of it north to Homs and Aleppo. He and his lieutenants hurried out, documents in hand, and mounted up.

Olden reached across to Bill and said tongue-in-cheek: 'Think of it, dear mighty Bill, you and I have just officially conquered Damascus and Syria.'

Bill's ears twitched, more from the flies than the awesome declaration.

Olden turned to his lieutenants. 'Bill is not impressed, but I hope you lot are. Your captain has joined a list of notables in history, including Egypt's Rameses II, Greece's Alexander and France's Napoleon.' The lieutenants were to be given the history lesson and reminded of their place in it.

Olden then looked back along the column. It was settled and ready to move off again. He patted Bill and said: 'Let's see if we can collect some more Turks.'

26

A BULLET WITH BILL'S NAME ON IT

Shanahan tore open the large parcel. He was surprised and then confused to find the carved figurine of Bill that he had given Cath Phelan. With it was a note from her husband Bob Kerr. He introduced himself and then wrote:

I am very sorry to have to inform you Cath died a week ago from lung cancer. She wanted me to return this wonderful horse sculpture to you. Clearly she was very fond of you. She insisted on calling our son after you. Michael is a bonny lad of nearly eighteen months, which is the hardest part of this tragedy. He will never really know what a stunning, vibrant wonderful woman his mother was. Cath told me about you and your record at Romani, and the stories about that amazing horse. I heard about Bill winning the Jericho

*Cup. A Sumner Reed wrote a great newspaper feature
about it. Incredible! You must be mighty proud to have
trained and befriended such a God-Given Gift to our cause.*

Shanahan put the letter down and wiped away tears just as
Charlotte entered the room.

'Darlin', what's wrong?'

Shanahan pointed to the letter lying on the lounge-
room table next to Bill's replica. Charlotte read it.

'Oh, my sweet, I am sorry,' she said. 'Was she a close
friend?'

'Someone I knew in Cairo.'

'She named her son after you . . .?'

Shanahan shrugged.

Charlotte rubbed her stomach. She was due to give
birth in a few weeks.

'Does this mean,' she said slowly, 'that if it's a boy I can
call it Stanley?'

'No son of my mine will be called that,' he said with
a scowl.

'Why not?'

'Too English. Besides, I don't expect any son of mine
to be a butler.'

'Very funny.' She sat in his lap, being careful to avoid
his stump. She kissed him lightly on the forehead and
wiped away tears from his cheeks. 'It wouldn't matter if
Stanley was a middle name, would it, darlin'?'

The child was a girl, which avoided any immediate
arguments about names. They called her Audrey Eileen

Patricia. She was born on 31 October 1918, an auspicious date marking the armistice in the Middle East War and victory for Chauvel's Desert Mounted Column. It had liberated Arab states and regions by driving the Turks out of the Middle East for the first time in 400 years.

The end of the desert conflict, however, triggered a certain disharmony, especially when the Anzac force learned the official word that most of the horses were to be shot or sold wherever the British government wished.

Early in November 1918, Banjo Paterson and Aidan Sutherland had the unenviable task of leading 128 horses out into the desert a kilometre from an oasis. There they met the captain of a machine-gun squadron. The horses were bunched into rows of six in front of twelve gunners, who were lined up on a knoll before the mounts. Paterson on Blackham and Sutherland on Penny stood to one side.

'This is the worst thing I've ever seen,' Sutherland said softly.

'I feel like a mass murderer,' Paterson said with a grimace. 'I can't watch this. C'mon, let's get back to the depot.'

The two men galloped off and did not look back as the machine-guns opened up and felled all the horses. A few minutes later they heard intermittent revolver shots as the gunners moved among the mounts looking for survivors of the machine-gun volley.

Later in the day, another squadron of horses was trotted out of the depot for their last ride after a feed and watering. This time Paterson and Sutherland could not bear to accompany them. Paterson sat at his desk for several minutes before he called Sutherland to the office.

'Aidan, I can't cope with this anymore,' he said. 'I quit. You are in charge.'

'I should go too,' Sutherland replied, 'it's a poisoned chalice.'

'You can't go,' Paterson said, 'someone has to run this bloody death camp.'

'Stay a wee while, please, Major. It's your duty.'

In despair, Bow Legg wrote to Shanahan on 2 November:

It is an awful, awful thing! These fine old comrades carried us faithfully under all sorts of hardships. You'll remember that terrible march to Oghratina, when we found the butchered British cavalry. The bloody Sinai sand was tough going, and some of us would never have made it but for Bill; you missed the rides through the Judean Hills. That was no fun for man or beast. The hardest of all were those long, exhausting treks across the Jordan and up the goat tracks of the Mountains of Moab. The horses often went without water for days. I haven't even bothered to mention the battles we took them into and how brave they were, as you know better than anyone! Now the authorities want to dispose of them like some worthless trash! I don't know what we will do. Mullagh says he can't hand Bill in, but he will have to. Some of the blokes are taking matters into their own hands and are riding them into the desert and shooting them. Mullagh is thinking of doing that. Our mate Chook has got malaria and is on his way home. At least he is spared the horse problem. I don't know what to do myself. I can't sleep thinking about it. I'll let you know what transpires. Not good news my old peg-leg mate! I hope you are appreciating your newborn. Life is so precious. Cherish it.

The letter depressed Shanahan. Charlotte wanted to know what was wrong with him but he would not say. She didn't understand how he could be so happy with his baby daughter one day, and in a black mood the next. He shut himself in his study and would not come out. Then Charlotte found Legg's letter and knew what had triggered his anguish while not fully understanding its impact.

*

Paterson responded to Sutherland's plea and stayed a few days more, but he could not stand the shrinking of his once-mighty remount numbers. Both men were shattered by the experience and a pall of gloom settled on the Moascar depot. Trainers and staff began to leave as their duties were reduced.

'I have so many wee pals amongst the neddies,' Sutherland said as he and Paterson wandered down to the stables, 'it is so, so sad to see them sent to their maker this way. I liked them all, wi' no favourites, except for Penny. I've grown to love that wee mare as much as Bill does!' He paused then remarked: 'At this rate the only horse apart from your thoroughbreds to make it back to Australia will be Sandy, Colonel Bridges' mount.'

'My thoroughbreds are being taken today,' Paterson said despondently. When Sutherland looked shocked, he added, 'No, not to be destroyed, Sergeant. Allenby has ordered them back to England for cavalry service.'

'But you own them!'

'Not according to British laws of acquisition in war time. But I will fight the army in the courts on this, if I can afford it!' He sighed. 'But it's the last straw for me. I am resigning. I will take a boat to Sydney next week.'

This left Sutherland in charge of the remount depot, which promised to be empty by the end of November. More directives from High Command administration reached the depot. More than 20,000 horses were to be sold to the Egyptians. Others were luckier. They would go to the British and Indian armies. If the horses were more than twelve years old, they were to be put down officially. Their parts—hides, manes, tails and horseshoes—were to be sold. Troopers were disgusted by the idea of their younger mounts being sold into Middle Eastern markets. They had witnessed the way the locals in Egypt, Palestine and Syria treated their animals, and how emaciated and flogged their horses were. Be damned, they exclaimed, if they were going to leave them to a life like that.

Every day Sutherland turned a blind eye to hundreds of troopers taking their mounts into the desert and shooting them rather than see them sold or face an anonymous machine-gun firing squad. This act was repeated from Moascar to every Light Horse camp along the Mediterranean coast as far as Rafa. It was the most awful moment of the entire war for most troopers. They had seen the result of massacres by Turks and Arabs. They had lost good mates in battle. But nothing compared to the moment they felt compelled to end the lives of their mounts, who were their closest cobbers. Many had dreamt of riding them down the main street of their town or city in a parade celebrating their historic victory over the Turks. Suddenly, all that reverie had turned to dust. How many of these men would wake in the middle of a nightmare experiencing the feel, smell and look of their horses, and then the sound of the shot, the sight of the buckle of the knees and the further sensation of the dull thud on the sand?

Trooper Oliver Hogue (using the pseudonym 'Trooper Bluegum') wrote a poem, 'The Horses Stay Behind', reflecting the emotions of the Light Horsemen in its fourth and fifth verses:

I don't think I could stand the thought of my old fancy hack
Just crawling round old Cairo with a 'Gyppo on his back.
Perhaps some English tourist out in Palestine may find
My broken-hearted Waler with a wooden plough behind.

No: I think I'd better shoot him and tell a little lie:—
'He floundered in a wombat hole and then lay down
*   to die.'*
May be I'll get court-martialled; but I'm damned if
*   I'm inclined*
To go back to Australia and leave my horse behind.

*

On 13 November Sutherland opened a letter addressed to the absent Paterson from Shanahan, pleading with him to spare Bill. Sutherland went down to the stables and found Penny was the only one of the special mounts left. Bill had gone. Sutherland made enquiries. Not one member of the dwindling depot staff could tell him.

Finally a young trainer said: 'You'd better ask Jackie Mullagh.'

'What's that mean, laddie?'

'He's gone for a ride on Bill out to the oasis,' the trainer said. 'He had his rifle with him.'

Sutherland felt ill. He wandered back to his office and tried to occupy himself by opening more of the pile of mail addressed to Paterson, which had to be attended to. A letter from General Chauvel had him sitting up in his chair. It requested that 'ten pack mules and/or horses be retained for a mission to Gallipoli. They will accompany a special Anzac Light Horse Contingent to collect artefacts and memorabilia for the Australian National Memorial Collection [later the first collection of the Australian War Memorial].'

Sutherland cupped his hands to his face. His brain raced. He looked at his watch. He called in the young trainer.

'When exactly did Jackie take off wi' Bill?' Sutherland asked.

'Jeez, I dunno, Aidan, an hour ago, maybe a little less?'

'Bugger!' Sutherland exclaimed. 'Saddle up a neddie for me, will you please? But not wee Penny. I don't want her to witness this.'

Mullagh had not ridden Bill to the oasis. He had taken another horse and Bill was led there. He was accompanied by Legg on his mount that he had been with for three years.

'I can't shoot mine,' Legg confessed as they reached the oasis, 'I haven't got the stomach for it. I'm handing him in tomorrow. I'll let the gunners do it. He'll go down with about a hundred others in one spray of their bloody weapons!'

Mullagh said nothing as he tethered Bill to a palm tree behind a mound.

'Gunna give him one last drink?' Legg asked.

'He had a good last feed and a drink at the depot,' Mullagh said sullenly.

He put bullets in his rifle, placed it down on the sand and went over to Bill, stroking his mane. The horse pulled his head away as if he was rejecting the sentimentality and saying *get on with it*. Mullagh wanted to say something to him but couldn't. He returned to collect his rifle and took up a position five metres from Bill. Legg looked away. He heard the rifle being cocked. He waited ten seconds, fifteen seconds, thirty seconds . . . Legg was just about to look back when he heard the shot ring out.

Sutherland pushed his horse harder than ever before through the retarding sand and over hilly dunes until he was in sight of the small oasis. Vultures circled overhead.

The number of animal carcasses being left in the desert was drawing them to the area and providing them with a daily banquet. He heard a shot.

Sutherland mouthed an expletive to himself—'I'm too late!' he said—but kept pushing the horse in the hope that the shot had not been fired by Mullagh. As he approached the modest oasis of six trees and one well, he could see a man sitting in the sand holding his head in his hands. It was Mullagh. Legg was standing over him, handing him something. A horse was tethered at the oasis. It belonged to Legg.

Where is Bill? Sutherland wondered as he barrelled up to the two men. Dismounting, he saw the huge horse tethered to a solitary tree behind a mound.

'You're not allowed to destroy him,' Sutherland said.

'Fuck off, Aidan!' Mullagh mouthed. 'I've gotta bloody do it!' He took a swig from a whisky flask that Legg had given him. 'Couldn't do it a few minutes back, but now I've got some Dutch courage . . .'

Sutherland handed him the letter from Chauvel. As Mullagh ran his eyes over it, Sutherland took his rifle and emptied it.

'What the fuck's this mean?' Mullagh protested. 'I've still got to do it sooner or later.'

'No you don't,' Sutherland said, wandering over to Bill. 'I've got an idea.'

A short time later, Sutherland accompanied eight pack mules and four horses—including Bill and Penny—by train to a wharf at Rafa on the coast. They were part of the contingent on the artefact-gathering trip to Gallipoli. He and a fellow sergeant counted the animals as they walked up a gangplank to a merchant ship destined for Gallipoli.

'There you are, Sergeant, ten mules and horses as requisitioned by General Chauvel,' Sutherland said, showing him the letter.

'There were twelve animals, weren't there?' the sergeant said, frowning and glancing back at the rumps of the last two mules being pushed up the gangplank.

'No, no, ten,' Sutherland said innocently, 'only ten.'

The sergeant was about to dispute the number when Sutherland shook hands firmly. The sergeant felt something paper-like in his palm. It was a five-pound note. He pocketed it as Sutherland said, 'Now I'll be coming back wi' those ten animals in a couple of weeks.' He smiled and added: 'We can count the ten coming off, just to make sure the Turks haven't nicked any of them.' He winked, picked up a backpack and hurried up the gangplank.

It was an emotional moment for Sutherland and the other handpicked 199 Anzac troopers who returned to Gallipoli after nearly three years. They wandered daily with the pack animals from Anzac Cove up into the hills, jagged ridges and ravines, searching for the remains of troopers and diggers who lay where they had been felled on the Nek, Dead Man's Ridge and all the other chillingly but aptly named trenches in or closer to the Turks' former strongholds. Their remains would be placed in properly marked graves.

On the first night, Sutherland took aside Kenan Kelic, a Turkish interpreter, former soldier and POW. He was acting as a liaison with people in the villages, who were a little surprised to see the foreign invaders returning.

'Could we find a local blacksmith or horse-owner?' Sutherland asked. 'I'd like to sell a couple of the horses . . .'

The next morning, the two men rode with Bill and Penny in tow to a small village behind nearby Suvla Bay. They found the village elder, Ahmed, a toothless, pleasant, middle-aged man. The three men chatted for a while. Ahmed offered coffee. He examined the two horses. Soon a group of eight villagers had joined them to marvel at Bill. There was some animation among them.

'One of them thinks he knows Bill,' Kelic interpreted. 'Did he ever do the despatch run?'

'Yes.'

'One of them claims to have shot at him. They are all very impressed.' Kelic smiled. 'This village will be a good home for them.'

After a few minutes, the village elder approached them.

'He has never seen a more magnificent animal than Bill,' Kelic told Sutherland, 'but he could not afford them.'

'Does he want them? Penny is a good foaler, tell him.'

'I've told him.'

'How much can he afford?'

The two Turks chatted.

'In English money, it is five pounds.'

'Will he really look after them?'

'Oh yes, he'll take Bill for himself and his grandson . . .'

'But they mustn't mount him. Tell him he must use him only as a packhorse and a stud. Make that clear.'

'I already have.'

The village elder went to hand the money to Sutherland.

'No,' he said with a smile, 'tell him they are a gift from Australia.'

The Turks were most grateful.

Kelic and Sutherland trotted off. As they reached the top of a hill overlooking the village, they glanced back. A small crowd, including some women, now surrounded the two horses. The villagers were making a fuss of the two Walers, who seemed already content in their new home.

Aidan Sutherland smiled and mumbled to himself: 'Can't wait to write to Shanahan and Mullagh.'

27

EPILOGUE

Michael Shanahan, Charlotte and their two children (Audrey and Michael Stanley, who was born in 1919) arrived at Withersfield, in the gem mining territory of central Queensland, early in 1920. The train took them to a cattle loading depot at the end of the line. They had little money and so decided to make the depot their home to start with. It was a stark new beginning but the resourceful Shanahan overcame his disability and financial challenges by applying himself to fresh circumstances with his usual 'can-do' philosophy. He and Charlotte had another four children and moved to Brisbane, where Shanahan found long-term employment as a lift operator at Finney Isles department store.

In 1946, after some twenty-eight years of marriage, Charlotte left him and her children and returned to

London to again be with Stanley Butler, whose first wife had died. Shanahan, then seventy-six, battled on, beloved and cared for by his children and, later, his grandchildren. He stayed super-fit and rode a horse until he was eighty-four. He always hobbled along with his sticks at every Anzac Day parade, where his men showed him the utmost respect. Lieutenant Mulherin and the rest of his squadron always referred to him as 'the Major'.

Michael Shanahan died at age ninety-four on 12 October 1964. His association with Bill the Bastard caused him to become a permanent part of the Anzac legend.

And what of the Bastard himself? He is commemorated in a bronze statue at the village of Murrumburrah, nestled in undulating hills 340 kilometres south-west of Sydney and 125 kilometres north-west of Canberra. The sculpture, by local artist Carl Valerius, is entitled 'Retreat from Romani'. The life-sized work depicts Bill carrying Shanahan and the other four troopers to safety in the action that earned Shanahan the DSO.

Over the decades, some visitors to Gallipoli who know of Bill the Bastard have taken time to visit the tiny village behind Suvla Bay where Bill and his mate Penny lived out their days. Nearly a century after the end of the Great War, Australians swear they have seen some extraordinary horses in the area that look suspiciously like sizeable Walers.